BRUCE DAVIDSON

World Champion of Eventing

with Sally O'Connor, Akhtar Hussein,
and Caroline Silver

HOUGHTON MIFFLIN COMPANY BOSTON   1980

IRISH CAP — WORLD CHAMPION 1974

ABOVE: Dressage.
LEFT: Over a cross-country drop fence, Ledyard, Mass., 1978.
BELOW: Stadium jumping.

ISBN 0-395-29117-8
Library of Congress Catalogue Card Number: 80-13889
Printed in the United States of America. M 10 9 8 7 6 5 4 3 2 1

The Davidson stable colors are red and yellow.

BELOW LEFT: Might Tango, Bruce Davidson, and son Buck.
BELOW: Irish Cap, Might Tango, and Carol Davidson, Bruce Davidson, Nancy and Buck Davidson.

Mark Phillips (GB) on Columbus, jumping into the Trout Hatchery at Burghley World Championships 1974. The horse has jumped awkwardly and left both hind legs on the rail. The rider has slipped his reins to give the horse a chance to recover his balance.

LEFT TO RIGHT ABOVE: Helmut Rethemeier (FRG) on Ladalco, over the head of the lake, Kentucky 1978. The horse has made an energetic leap and is sailing into the lake. Rider has a good position over the center of balance and is ready to help the horse on landing. Richard Meade (GB) on Bleak Hills, traversing the lake.
RIGHT: The US riders at Kentucky study the lake complex with Jack LeGoff.

Bruce Davidson (USA) on
Irish Cap, at the Trout
Hatchery, Burghley 1974.
Perfect balance and con-
trol, complete confidence
of horse and rider. Horse
is fresh and on his toes,
looking on to the next
fence.

LEFT TO RIGHT ABOVE: Michael Plumb
(USA) on Laurenson, showing a fresh
horse with a lot of scope jumping well
over the fourth lake element. Jack
LeGoff, coach of the USET Three-Day
Team.
RIGHT: James Wofford (USA) on Carawich, over the last cross-country fence
in Kentucky 1978.

ABOVE: Tad Coffin (USA), gold medalist at the 1976 Olympics, on Karama Kazuri over the first of two banks, Radnor 1978.
ABOVE RIGHT: Lucinda Prior-Palmer trots out Village Gossip for the veterinary inspection, Kentucky 1978.
RIGHT: Michael Plumb (USA) on Better and Better, over the tiger trap at Blue Ridge 1978.
BELOW: Caroline Treviranus (USA) on Comic Relief, riding in her second world championship, Kentucky 1978.
BELOW RIGHT: The Selection Committee, including Jack LeGoff, seriously considers Might Tango as a candidate for Kentucky after his brilliant performance at Chesterland, August 1978.

Might Tango — World Champion 1978

ABOVE: Bruce Davidson and Might
Tango win the Gladstone Trophy at
Chesterland 1978.

ABOVE: Bruce Davidson on Irish Cap
accepts the World Championship trophy from H.R.H. Prince Philip, Duke
of Edinburgh, at Burghley 1974.
LEFT: The Duke of Edinburgh seems
reluctant to relinquish the World
Championship trophy to Bruce Davidson on Might Tango, Kentucky 1978.

TO CAROL

Acknowledgments

With thanks to the Davidson family and friends for the photographs of Bruce with Shirlore and Cecil, riding team horses at Gladstone, and performing dressage in Kentucky;

to Jack LeGoff for the photograph of Image;

and to the following photographers: P. Lynch, three early pictures of Irish Cap; Jack Dewell, Caroline Treviranus on Cajun; W. Ernst, Irish Cap in the ring at Burghley; Findlay Davidson, Irish Cap on Burghley cross-country and Carol Davidson at Badminton; *The Eventer,* Irish Cap in early competition; Sunshine Photo, Paddy at South Hamilton; Terry Bramham, Kentucky photos of LeGoff in the golf cart, Might Tango on steeplechase and at Fort Lexington, and receiving his awards; Fae Hapgood, dressage by J. J. Babu and Sunrise;

also to Joseph Martin, for the drawings of the Kentucky cross-country jumps; and to Christine Bousfield for the diagrams.

Preface

Any book about an international athlete necessarily takes shape in many places. The action moves from important competition to important competition with a few brief shining moments spent in the spotlight at the awards ceremonies. These shining moments pass in the wink of an eye with few of the applauding crowd giving a thought to the hours, weeks, months, even years of dedicated, persistent preparation that lie behind the victory smile.

Indeed, it takes years to produce a world class performer, with sweat and pain being more natural to the competitor than the plaudits of the crowd. In equestrian sports the strain is doubled as not only the human, but the equine athlete must reach perfection together. When Bruce Davidson and Irish Cap won the World Championships title at Burghley, England in 1974, he was a new star who had rocketed into prominence with the entire American team coached so ably by Jack LeGoff. For the next four years Bruce proved conclusively that his success was more than the brief appearance of a comet, and in 1978 he did what no other rider has done, he defended his world title by winning a second individual championship in Lexington, Kentucky.

Akhtar Hussein had been following the international three-day event circuit through the decade of the 1970s, recording in his superb photographs the fortunes and misfortunes of the world's top riders and horses, and as a result he acquired a great many pictures of Bruce and his horses. The idea of a book on the World Champion came naturally, and he proposed such a book in the spring of 1978, before the competition in Kentucky.

The nucleus of the book was the photographic record, but the words that would provide the text needed to be collected together and set down on paper, and Akhtar kindly asked if I would help to do so.

The championship year was a busy one for Bruce, and it was not until after his victory in Lexington that he could consider working on a book.

In the spring of 1979, Bruce and I began a weekly taping session, spending night after night feeding his ideas, memories, and words into a tape recorder. We sat in the Davidson's living room covering a different subject every night, punctuated by conversations with the two children, Buck and Nancy. We reminisced about horses, riders, and competitions, with Carol Davidson filling in gaps when our memory failed. We finished with a pile of tapes about two feet high — enough for several books. They were transcribed and sorted into the actual chapters, with Caroline Silver lending her expertise in creating a flowing effective manuscript.

Akhtar made several trips to Chesterland Farm to photograph the champion in his everyday routines of training and preparing for competition.

This book, then, is about Bruce Davidson, World Champion, and his two horses, Irish Cap and Might Tango, and although it is written in the third person it contains, on the whole, the champion's own words.

And we all join in thanking our editor, Ruth Hapgood, and other good friends at Houghton Mifflin Company, and Joan Fulton of Harold Matson Company who brought us all together.

SALLY O'CONNOR

To Balquis and Dr. Elizabeth Green, the special thanks of the photographer; also to my brother Anwar and Anwar's wife Caroline; to Willie Smith, BBC photographer; to Peter Clarke, artist; to the many people who have encouraged me throughout the years in creating this book; and to all other partners of event riders whose selfless work behind the scenes makes champions possible.

AKHTAR HUSSEIN

Contents

Part III. World Championships 1978

I
World Championships 1974

1

The Challenger

So did this horse excel a common one
In shape, in courage, colour, pace and bone
SHAKESPEARE, *Venus and Adonis*

I

It was snowing heavily on the morning of February 7, 1974, when Bruce and Carol Davidson set out on the drive to the Department of Agriculture's quarantine station at John F. Kennedy airport. Behind them in the red-and-yellow four-horse van Irish Cap and Paddy, good travelers both, pulled placidly at their haynets, cushioned against the freezing air by the piles of tack trunks and suitcases stacked around their stalls. Irish Cap was Bruce's horse and Paddy was Carol's, and they were all about to set off across the Atlantic for a nine-month stay. The quantity of baggage needed for their proposed assault on the British domination of three-day events was immense, and it had taken them and their grooms, Barbara Curtis and Ann Geoghegan, many hours to load.

Bruce and Carol had been married for only a month, but they had planned this trip long before. They had first met while working at the United States Equestrian Team's headquarters in Gladstone, New Jersey — both of them promising young riders who had been selected for training by Jack LeGoff, the autocratic French cavalry officer who was coach to the American three-day event team. Bruce and Carol had talked then about making a trip to England to compete at Badminton, the most famous of all the individual three-day competitions and the one that every rider secretly would like to win. As the young riders' friendship deepened into love, Bruce proposed to Carol that a trip to Badminton in the spring of 1974 would be a splendid extended honeymoon and would give them a chance to qualify for the World Championships team for that fall. They were married on January 5.

The journey to the quarantine station took longer than expected on the snowy roads, and in the raw wind icicles swung from trees along Interstate 95. Later, the magnificent outlines of Manhattan were blurred in a moving cloud of white. It was almost dark when Bruce pulled the van into the airport grounds and led the horses down the ramp and into small, squalid stalls that smelled dankly of stale urine from countless

OPPOSITE: Bruce and Carol ride out for a training session.

3

animals, all potential disease carriers, which had been quarantined there. It was no place for a honeymoon. Concerned for the horses' peace of mind in this strange, ill-smelling place, Bruce and Carol spent an uncomfortable night curled up on a pile of horse blankets beside their stalls.

In the morning Irish Cap and Paddy were loaded into box containers and hoisted aboard the huge jet plane by a hydraulic forklift. A group of small polo ponies headed for Germany and a herd of Quarter Horses bound for Australia via compulsory quarantine in England joined the two big event horses for the flight. The Davidsons settled into the special seats for passengers accompanying livestock, ready to feed their charges hay to keep their ears from popping during the pressure of take-off, but both horses were unperturbed when the aircraft lifted noisily off the runway and climbed above the gray snow clouds.

The flight was uneventful, as most horse flights are. Lulled by the monotonous roar of the engines, Irish Cap and Paddy chewed calmly on hay from the haynets which hung in front of them, dozing off from time to time against the padded linings of their stalls. Thirty-five thousand feet below this temporary stable the Atlantic ocean rolled in storm, but all the Davidsons could see was an unbroken bed of white cloud cover. They took the opportunity to catch up on some sleep.

Bruce slept in snatches, caught between dream and dream-reality. For as long as he could remember he had had horse fever. Even as a kid all he had thought of had been riding — riding to the width and depth of his potential; riding on a par with the best in the world. It was this need that had led him to the selection trials held in 1970 for the three-day team, choosing this form of horse sport over all others because the event rider has to be an all-rounder, expert in three demanding disciplines, and therefore as nearly as possible the complete horseman. For three years thereafter he had been LeGoff's willing pupil, obeying orders without question — watching, learning, sweating, shivering, taking fear and pain in silence, completely submissive to his coach — because he wanted to learn. He wanted to learn not necessarily with the ambition of riding in the Olympic Games, or even of receiving acclaim in any way, but because there was nothing else he would rather do. Now, high over the Atlantic, he was for the first time on his own, free to make his own decisions and to plan his own strategies. He felt excited and nervous.

On the wet tarmac at London's Heathrow airport a hired horse box waited to take the young Americans to Wylye, Wiltshire, where Lord and Lady Hugh Russell had offered them the use of their impressive training facilities on the edge of Salisbury Plain. The young couple were to live in a small cottage belonging to National Hunt trainer Ian Dudgeon, in the nearby village of Chitterne and here they unpacked their abundant gear as quickly as possible, anxious to get settled into their regular training routine. Apart from the usual work with Irish Cap and Paddy, the days ahead were to include riding out at dawn each morning on Ian's racehorses to build up their own legs and lungs for the physical demands of riding round Badminton, because a three-day rider has to require the same standard of fitness of himself as of his horse. On top of this Bruce insisted that they stick to a diet of small breakfast, no lunch, and one-course dinner, which would not be every bride's image of a honeymoon.

Bruce and Irish Cap at the start of their long partnership in 1970.

The countryside at Wylye lends itself to fitting up a horse. The steep, rolling hills are ideal for putting on muscle in long, slow workouts, and the well-established turf is perfect for galloping stretches to sharpen up the wind. Itself the site of an annual three-day event, Wylye has every conceivable type of cross-country obstacle somewhere on its grounds, and banks, ditches, brushes, drop fences, water obstacles, and oxers of all heights and widths gave Bruce and Carol a fine variety of practice. Using the interval training methods taught by LeGoff, Irish Cap and Paddy steadily got fit for the competitions ahead.

The schedule of daily work had been precisely planned so that the horses would reach peak fitness at Badminton, which was to take place on April 25–28. Before leaving America, Bruce and Carol had filled in their entry blanks and sent them in along with their licenses from the American Horse Shows Association (the official national federation that must give permission before U.S. riders can enter international competitions) and the passports for the two horses. The only possible vicissitudes which now stood between them and competition at Badminton were the physical setbacks which can happen to any horse or rider during even the most careful training program.

Badminton was Bruce's first goal that year. His second was the World Championships, also to be held in England — at Burghley Park, Lincolnshire, in September — though his selection as a possible candidate for the American team at Burghley depended entirely upon a good performance at Badminton. He had to prove that Irish Cap, whose talents against North American horses were known, was also capable of competing with the best in Europe.

Irish Cap had never looked or gone as well as he did that spring. In 1973 he had undergone an operation to improve his wind. Veterinary surgeons had fastened back a flap of partially paralyzed tissue in the windpipe with a special suture so that the flow of air was uninterrupted. A side result of this operation was that Irish Cap had become more susceptible to disease, but his intake of air had been dramatically improved so that he could now gallop effortlessly for miles. He was lean, hard, and fitter than he had ever been.

February was wet, March was wetter, and Carol began to long for the clear skies of home. "It would be easy to be a weather forecaster in England," she said. "All you have to do is wake up and predict rain and you'll be right!" April in sharp contrast began with a three-week drought and the ground became as hard as iron. Yet concern over the hard going did not take away from the thrill that the two young Americans felt on first arriving at Badminton House. When the horses were settled into the great stable yard attached to the huge stone pile which is home to the Duke of Beaufort, Bruce and Carol set out eagerly for their first look at the cross-country course.

The course was built in the vast deer park which surrounds the house. It undulated through the avenues of mature trees which radiate from the

Princess Anne, watched closely by her mother the Queen, confers with her trainer Alison Oliver at the Windsor Horse Trials in 1974.

The Queen and Queen Mother at Badminton in 1974.

The Queen, Queen Mother, and other members of the royal family watch intently as the horses are jogged out at the veterinary inspection in the stable-yard at Badminton 1974.

RIGHT: Mark Phillips on Columbus jumping into the water at Badminton 1974.

Carol Davidson rides Paddy over the Tiger Trap at Badminton 1974.

massive building, wound through the woods, looped down in front of the forecourt through the ornamental lake, and finished up in front of the huge complex of trade stands by the main arena. Centuries of husbanding had created perfect turf, ideal for the galloping hooves of the world's best horses. The immense fences awed the young couple. "*This* is what it's all about," said Bruce as they walked round. "This really *is* a complete test of horse and rider — they're going to have to be both bold *and* clever."

As in every major three-day event, the competition at Badminton is stretched over four days. The first two days are given up to dressage, which takes so long to judge because the judges only study one horse at a time and each competitor performs individually. After that comes the thrilling day of the speed and endurance, divided into three early phases — roads and tracks, steeplechase, and roads and tracks — and culminating in the fearsome cross-country phase at the end of many miles of riding. The final day, the show jumping test, passes quickly, since at every top-level event there are many competitors who retire or who are eliminated during the speed and endurance. The winner is the horse who has shown himself to be, in total, most obedient to and harmonious with his rider (dressage), most brave and clever and enduring (speed and endurance), and most willing and able to make a further effort after an exhausting day's work (show jumping). The show jumping test is not a test of jumping ability, which has been proved on the cross-country course, but of soundness of body and greatness of heart.

Despite the challenge from many international riders of high quality, the first phase of the competition, the dressage, was won very easily by Princess Anne on Doublet, the horse on which she had been European Champion in 1971, with an amazingly low score of only 29.33 penalty points. Bruce and Irish Cap placed seventh in this section, which put them well in the running with the rigors of the cross-country ahead, and Carol, riding Paddy, was up in the top third of the contestants.

On Saturday, cross-country day, over 160,000 people thronged the grounds of Badminton House. The approach roads were jammed with cars for hours before the first horse was due on the course. Since eventing in America was only just beginning to become popular, Bruce and Carol were totally unprepared for such crowds. In England, however, the presence of the royal family, who always stayed at Badminton House for the event, plus the participation of Princess Anne as a competitor, had turned the sport into a national television attraction. Some of the people came to watch the horses, some to catch a glimpse of the royal family, and some to enjoy a day's outing in the country. Most of them brought their dogs.

Carol was to go well before Bruce, and, when the starter's white flag dropped, she set out confidently on Paddy, who was moving well within himself. Unfortunately they had got only as far as the eleventh fence, the Keeper's Rails, when Paddy decided that he had had enough for that day and refused out. Eventing is so often like that: all the months of hope and preparation lost in a few short moments at one obstacle. Bitterly disappointed, Carol returned to the stables to help Bruce get ready with Irish Cap.

Though Irish Cap had never jumped a course of this size before, he handled the immense fences with ease, meeting the challenge with confidence in himself and in his rider. At the Quarry, a fence with tight distances and short strides, Bruce had an anxious moment when Irish Cap chose to jump big and bold and consequently nearly fell. As he made a quick recovery, Bruce thought to himself, "I certainly hope you learned something from that, Cap." Cap had: he made no more mistakes, galloping on so strongly that when Bruce glanced at his watch as they crossed the finish line he was elated to see that they had eight seconds in hand.

Yet, when the official time was posted on the score board, Bruce was down as having incurred 13.6 time faults. There had been, it seemed, a discrepancy in the times posted at the Briefings of Competitors. Deeply unhappy because he knew that Irish Cap could easily have run round in a faster time if he had thought it was necessary, Bruce lodged an official protest. He could see from the scoreboard that other riders had suffered from the same mistake on the part of the organizers. For example, the British riders Chris Collins and Mark Phillips had ridden two horses each and had obviously learned from their scores on the first horses that the time was wrong. On their second horses they had gone faster and had no time penalties. Mark Phillips on Columbus, the big rangy gray horse belonging to the Queen, was one of the last to go and had taken the lead with a very fast time. Nonetheless, Bruce's protest was overruled.

After the third day's show jumping Columbus had won and Irish Cap had placed third. The thrill of competing at Badminton had been marred by Carol's elimination and the controversy over the time faults, and the Davidsons drove back to Wylye with mixed feelings. Still, Bruce was delighted with the way Irish Cap had gone, and that was the most important fact.

Consolation came in another form: knowing how meagerly the Davidsons had been eating, Sorrel Warwick, the cook at Wylye, threw a pudding party for them when they got home. After ten weeks on minimal rations, Bruce and Carol were given a choice of six different puddings plus lots of champagne.

II

Despite his good showing at Badminton, the selection committee in America thought it wise that Bruce return to the United States to ride in one of the official screening trials for the World Championships team. Bruce and Carol left the horses in the charge of their groom and flew back for the trials at Middletown, Delaware, where Bruce competed satisfactorily on Mrs. Charles Coles's Sparrowhawk. When Middletown was over the Davidsons returned at once to England to continue their training schedule and to help with the preparations for the rest of the American riders, who were to follow later in the year.

Up on the chalk downs at Wylye it was a fine, warm summer, not too hot and not too wet. Blue-winged butterflies fluttered around the horses' feet at exercise, and varieties of bird and plant life unknown in North America gave Bruce and Carol something new to see each day. Paddy's refusals at Badminton had knocked Carol out of any chance of riding in the World Championships, yet she took it bravely, delighting instead in watching her young husband's visible progress with Irish Cap and in acquiring the feel of life in an English country village, so like, and yet so foreign to, her native Pennsylvania.

On August 1 life changed drastically. Jack LeGoff with fourteen more horses and six riders arrived from America to prepare for the upcoming World Championships. Bruce and Carol's honeymoon was over.

LeGoff was pleased with Irish Cap's progress when Bruce proudly demonstrated what he had been working on. One of the biggest changes Bruce had made was to ride the horse in a double bridle for dressage work. He had experimented at the British Dressage Championships and had found that the big horse became more responsive and lighter in hand in a double, making him steady and precise.

A schedule of competitions for the horses and riders had been drawn up by LeGoff to help him to make his final selection of horse-rider combinations for the championships. With the exception of J. Michael Plumb, who had ridden for America in international competition since the Olympic Games in Rome in 1960, all the chosen riders were young and unknown, which did not matter at all to the coach provided he had matched the right horse to the right rider. Denny Emerson, Don Sachey, Beth Perkins, and Caroline Treviranus were all new faces to the English and to the rest of the world.

The Americans were not regarded as being any great threat to the long-established English supremacy in the sport, though word of their newfangled interval training system had spread as riders watched Bruce and Carol prepping for Badminton. Lucinda Prior-Palmer, one of the best young English riders, had been impressed enough by Irish Cap's performance to ask Bruce to draw up an interval training plan for her 1973 Badminton winner, Be Fair, and had adopted the system for herself, much to the derision of her compatriots. The English dislike change: when, at the turn of the century, the American jockey Tod Sloan had come over to England and had demonstrated, by the consistency with which he won races against his rivals, the efficacy of race-riding with short leathers, he had at first been laughed at as "a monkey up a stick." The laughter died quite quickly because there was nothing funny in always being beaten by Sloan, so British jockeys pulled up their leathers and raced against him on his own advantageous terms. But *interval training*! It had produced a third at Badminton — so what? Lucinda Prior-Palmer, who later became the most consistently brilliant performer in Europe on many different horses, was the sole English rider to feel that Bruce's training methods might help improve her own routine.

The Americans' final preparation for Burghley was the three-day event at Osberton, six weeks earlier. LeGoff decided that Bruce and Irish Cap, Mike Plumb and Good Mixture, Denny Emerson and Victor Dakin, Beth Perkins and Furtive, Don Sachey and Plain Sailing, and Caroline Treviranus and Cajun would be entered for a final tune-up.

Bruce and Irish Cap placed first in the dressage phase, thus upholding their growing reputation for style. The cross-country, though, was a disaster. LeGoff, as coach of the team, had given strict orders to each

Caroline Treviranus represented the United States in the World Championships at Burghley on Cajun.

individual on how to ride the course, and Bruce, who had been working alone for the past few months, found the transition back to riding to orders a difficult adjustment. Under orders to ride Irish Cap deliberately at a very slow speed, he tried hard to obey. He was nervous at the prospect of trying to hold the big, strong horse back, yet worried that he might jeopardize his chances of being part of the team if he refused to do as he had been told.

The fifth fence on the course was an option that could be taken either straight across the corner or in two jumps in and out. Bruce throttled his big horse down and tried to take the in-and-out, but Irish Cap, fighting for his head, gave a tremendous leap in and chested the second part. "Dammit!" thought Bruce, bitter with anger at having made a mistake. "I'd rather leave my horse *alone*." Resentment grew as he continued on course, trying to hold Irish Cap back only to have the horse jump poorly. "Don't hurt my Cap," he prayed.

One of the largest fences was a Normandy bank with a big triple bar on the top. Approaching at a slow speed, Irish Cap jumped up onto the bank, took a half-stride, and tried to jump out over the rails. He landed right on the middle rail, but fortunately he was able to continue.

A true fellowship of the horse exists in international eventing. Here Jane Starkey of Great Britain grooms for Torrance Watkins of the United States.

RIGHT: It would be no joke to slip on course. Special studs are screwed into the horse's shoes for traction on slippery ground.

At course's end, Bruce put the horse back into its stall and sat and cried, not because the chance of riding for his country seemed lost, but because of his love for his big, generous friend, the best horse in the world by his reckoning, who had gone badly because of the way he had been ridden. The drive back to Wylye seemed even longer than usual and was much more dismal.

The following day Irish Cap came out of his stable limping, but the riders had to leave Wylye to prepare for another event at Bramham, Yorkshire, with the less experienced horses. LeGoff insisted that Bruce leave Irish Cap behind to be cared for by someone else.

The psychology of coaching any great athlete is an art. Determining how much and just what kind of pressure to apply is part of the coach's success or failure. LeGoff is a master coach, a genius. Bruce, by nature, is quiet and passive; but he reacts to stress, he performs best when he feels his ability is in doubt, he competes hardest when he is challenged. LeGoff was forging a steely desire in the young rider to prove beyond any shadow of doubt that he was indeed the best. Bruce went to Bramham as ordered, rode Paddy around the course like a demon, and won.

By the time the riders arrived back at Wylye, Irish Cap's injury had proved to be minor and he was sound again. Bruce resumed his work, still smarting from the debacle at Osberton.

III

September 10 was the day of departure for Burghley. Bruce was out early in the Wylye stable yard, helping to load all the equipment into the rented horse boxes. He could not resist sneaking off for a look at Irish Cap, who was blooming, the bay coat shining like a well-polished mahogany table and the muscles on the hindquarters bulging with power. Sensing what was up, Irish Cap poked Bruce on the shoulder with his muzzle. Being an intelligent animal, he always knew when competitions were ahead because the change in stable routine alerted him; and, being also a conceited showman (the best disposition for a horse who performs in public), he reveled in the attention and the excitement. While the grooms led the horses up the lorry ramps, Bruce had a small conversation with himself: "*This is it* . . . I don't quite know what to expect; I guess it's like the first time I went up to Gladstone. I've dreamed of having my Irish Cap on the team way back since he was a baby, before I could even put him in hand . . ." Carol caught his eye, and he smiled and got into their car to follow the procession on the five-hour drive to Burghley.

During the drive into this challenging future, Bruce and Carol talked over the four years past that had led up to their current state of ecstatic suspense. A time in 1972 came back to Bruce, seeming much further away than a mere two years: LeGoff had told him then that if only he would loan his horse to Mike Plumb, Irish Cap could go to the Olympic Games. To which Bruce had replied, "It's not that I don't want my horse to go to the Olympics, but I have to do it *myself*." Well, now the time had come: he was going to do it himself.

The long-awaited arrival at Burghley was anticlimactic. A steady rain fell from a gray sky. The horses were stabled in portable tent stalls, ten feet by ten feet square, and the roofs leaked. Great big Irish Cap was so much squashed by his small stall that his head and shoulders hung out into the aisle; but his ears were pricked and his eyes shone with curiosity. He, at least, enjoyed the confusion.

Everyone helped to unload the equipment. Beth Perkins, carrying one end of a heavy tack trunk, slipped and dropped her end onto her foot. She was rushed off to hospital for X-rays, which showed that she had broken two small bones, but she was shortly back at the barn on crutches, determined to ride. "Riding isn't going to be so bad, I guess," she said, "but walking the course on crutches is going to give me calluses in the armpits." Her father took her boot to the local cobbler to have it slit open so that she would be able to slip it on over her bandages.

Riders from ten nations arrived throughout the day, filling the shed rows with commotion. The persistent rain kept most competitors under the roofs of their own allotted stables, and, despite a natural curiosity to inspect their rivals, the Americans stayed close together in the dry. LeGoff drew up a tight schedule of briefings.

Bruce was very conscious of the competition. He was especially aware of the British riders, who between them held most of the international prizes and who were now competing with the added advantage of being on their own ground. He watched Lucinda's yellow horse box for two roll in with Be Fair, and he watched Princess Anne's powerful new horse, Goodwill, and Mark Phillips's Columbus, the big gray who had beaten him at Badminton. Columbus was having precompetition nerves, and much work on a lunge line was needed to settle him down. Irish Cap, on the other hand, stood with his head in the aisle, enjoying the attention he attracted and inviting more of it. People were constantly passing through the stables, and Irish Cap said, as clearly as a horse can, "Hey! Come on over and give me a pat," while his teammate Good Mixture hid in the corner trying to ignore the crowd. Bruce felt that Irish Cap presented a diplomat's front, treating visitors to a friendly American welcome. In contrast, the Russian horses were secluded behind tarpaulins after a horrendous overland drive of several days, and no visitors were allowed in their section.

Bruce's emotions were wildly scrambled. He was trying to cope with the excitement and the pressures of his relationship with the coach and with his teammates. He found himself wavering: he wanted to look at the trade stands — but didn't want to look at the trade stands; he wanted to see the course, couldn't wait to see the course — but didn't want to see the course; he wanted to ride — but he didn't want to ride; he thought his horse was going well — but could go better. It was all so important, and now that the time had come he wanted the action to start. All his life he had wanted to have a horse like Cornishman V, the British 1970 World Champion three-day horse, and he felt that in Irish Cap he very probably had such a horse — if only he could prove it in the next few days. He had checked the statistics of the two former winners: Cornishman V had been ten years old, and Chalan, the Argentinian horse who had won the first World Championships in 1966, had also been ten years old. Irish Cap was exactly ten years old. Bruce knew in his heart that

OPPOSITE: Out of the water, Princess Anne in competition in 1974.

Irish Cap was the horse that everyone had to beat, but he couldn't tell anyone except Carol. And Carol already knew.

The American riders understood that this was first of all a team effort and that individual honors were secondary. An individual win *can* be written off as luck on the day, but a *team* victory proves national strength. The only other time that the United States had entered a team for a World Championships had been in 1966 (also held at Burghley), and the result had been a catastrophe — out of four of the team's riders only one had got through to the end of the competition and the team had been eliminated. If this was not enough to make the Americans feel that they must rise to Burghley with everything they had, LeGoff himself had competed there in 1963 on Laurier and had finished third, deprived at the last moment of first place by a single rail knocked down in stadium. Now he had broadcast the fact that his ambition was to beat the British; and not only that, but to beat them on their home soil.

Despite, or perhaps because of, these responsibilities, the Americans had a quiet air of confidence. They had selected six nice horses (four for the team, plus the two individual competitors allowed for each foreign country) and their coach had brought them to the peak of condition. With a bit of luck they might possibly show the Europeans how to play the game. LeGoff's fanatic attention to details, his merciless drilling of horse and rider in the basics of eventing, had prepared them to do their best.

The setting of the Championships overawed the Americans. The great house of the Cecil family, built in the sixteenth century of the warm, gray-gold local stone known as Barnack rag, and crowned with a fantastic profusion of turrets and spires, dominated the vast grounds. Designed around a central courtyard with an ornate clock tower, the Elizabethan house looks out over elaborately designed grounds laid out by Capability Brown, the most famous of all landscape gardeners, during twenty-five years of thought which began in 1754. Brown's genius in creating great open avenues might have been directed towards providing the ideal three-day event site. His vision of an ordered "natural" park provides today's course designers with copious opportunities to fit all sorts of strange obstacles into the varying terrain.

The official course inspection took place after the preliminary veterinary check on Wednesday. First, the competitors were driven around the roads and tracks phases in large commercial vehicles lent by Mercedes-Benz. The steeplechase course, set out on the erstwhile golf course, was seen to be open and inviting, but it was the anticipated inspection of the cross-country course, designed by Bill Thompson, that was mostly on the riders' minds.

As soon as they could politely get away, the Americans walked the cross-country course with Jack LeGoff. They were dumbfounded: nothing they had ever seen had prepared them for the reality of the massive course. From the fourth fence onwards the obstacles loomed over the riders as they approached on foot. "My God, it's big," Bruce said to Carol. "It's bigger than anything I ever dreamed of." It was the biggest course that any of them had ever seen, including even Mike Plumb, who had jumped more courses than anyone in the competition. But there it was; and jumped it must be. The American team went soberly back to the stables to consider their plan of attack.

After seeing that Irish Cap was settled, Bruce and Carol drove off to their hotel. Some of the horses that were left behind felt nervous in their foreign digs and were only picking at their feed, but not Irish Cap: he eagerly awaited Barbara Curtis with his meals, and as soon as he caught sight of her he made a strange trumpeting sound like an elephant. "Hooonh! Hooonh!" he called in greeting, having been unable to whinny like a normal horse since his wind operation. He was known as the "Heffalump," and the human members of his team, who were enthralled with his sound, frequently formed a line, head to tail, hunched over doing an "elephant walk," swaying down the aisle in front of Irish Cap's stall and trumpeting at him while he trumpeted back.

Since looking at the immense fences, LeGoff had decided that the four men, Mike Plumb, Don Sachey, Denny Emerson, and Bruce, would be the official team, while the two women, Beth with her broken foot, and Caroline, should ride as individuals. Following on from that was the vital decision of the riding order, and LeGoff had asked Mike and Bruce to help sort this out. The first rider is the one who has to get around and return to tell the others what to expect from the course, and LeGoff felt that Plain Sailing, ridden by Don Sachey, would get round no matter what, and that he should go first. Victor Dakin, Denny Emerson's horse, was new to international competition and was highly temperamental, especially in the dressage; but he was a catlike and clever jumper, and it was decided that he should go second. This left Bruce and Irish Cap and Mike and Good Mixture, a brilliant cross-country horse, to hold the team together (scores are taken from the best three) if Victor Dakin opted out. Now LeGoff asked for Bruce's evaluation of the two anchor horses — a curious sensation for the young rider, who was for the first time asked for an honest opinion. Despite the resentment that hung on from Osberton, Bruce felt very grateful for this consideration. He told LeGoff and Mike that he thought Irish Cap's chances in the dressage were excellent; probably better than those of Good Mixture, who could be difficult at times. He said that the two horses could probably run around the cross-country on an equal basis, but that Irish Cap might have a rail down in the show jumping, whereas Good Mixture could be counted on to go clean.

Traditionally, the last rider in each team is the one who is relied upon to be "cleanup man" — the one who rides to orders, the one who must sacrifice personal glory. His task entails taking no risky shortcuts and calls for steadiness if things have not gone well for another member of the team. Mike said that he didn't mind going last; in fact, that he was used to it. Thus the order of go was settled: Don Sachey with Plain Sailing, Denny Emerson with Victor Dakin, Bruce with Irish Cap, and Mike with Good Mixture.

To be brilliant in three-day eventing a rider needs to go all out and take chances. However, when one is riding as part of a team, discipline demands that the safety of the team comes first. Skill, experience, nerve, and ability, no matter how consummate, are always coupled with a certain amount of luck, and team riders must put the good of the team before their desire to shine as individuals. By accepting a team assignment, Bruce was therefore putting himself back under the coach's control, but this did not matter to him because, more than any individual glory for himself and for Irish Cap, he wanted the team to succeed. He wanted an American victory more than a Davidson victory.

When dinner was over the Davidsons sat in their room, unable to stop thinking about the competition ahead and the course. Bruce looked up at Carol from his armchair. "All those riders out there, all those Poles and Russians and the others," he said, "are going out to jump those fences. If all those people are going to do it, *I* can go out and do it in style. None of the others is sitting on an Irish Cap, so what the hell am I worrying about?" They got dressed and went out to the competitors' party, at which everyone participated in the donkey racing, and Bruce began to feel relaxed and at ease before the serious business of the contest. Colonel Bill Lithgow, the British coach, fell off a donkey and broke his ribs, which left him sore and slightly short of breath throughout the Championships.

IV

In the three busy days between first seeing the course and riding it, Bruce walked the complex route three times. He worried about the footing, which was soft in spots because of the persistent drizzle; yet, as he studied each massive fence, he thought about his horse, and in his heart he was confident that this was Irish Cap's type of course, suited to the big, bold jumper. The tension, the hectic conflict of personalities, seemed unimportant as his confidence and pride in his Irish Cap solidified.

One fence drew Bruce back several times to study his riding plan. It was the smallest fence of all, a little sloping ramp on top of a bank overlooking a sunken road. Bruce worried about it because Irish Cap liked to gallop with a long stride, jumping out over his fences boldly, and at a tiny fence like this he couldn't afford to come in fast because they might overjump and land in a heap on the road at the bottom. The water fence also looked treacherous, because the approach to it was down a steep slope that would become slippery if the rain continued and because there was a big vertical to jump over into a pond of murky water of uncertain depth. This, Bruce knew, would need a courageous horse.

Between walking the course, riding Irish Cap, and watching Don Sachey and Plain Sailing, Denny Emerson and Victor Dakin, and Beth Perkins and Furtive perform their tests, Bruce found that Thursday, the first day of dressage, passed quickly. When the competition was over and the crowds had driven home, Bruce walked back through the quiet parkland to say goodnight to Irish Cap. The wise bay head was buried in its feed bucket, oblivious to the tensions.

Bruce woke early on Friday, the second day of dressage competition and the first of his own performance. He dressed with care. Superstitious to the extreme, he always dressed from the left side first, putting his left arm or left leg into each garment before his right and buttoning or tying things left over right. When he made a mistake in the order of dressing he undid everything and started again until he was happy. Satisfactorily clothed, he set off for the stables thinking about the day ahead, the whole of it seemingly telescoped into the seven and one-half minutes it would take to perform his test. "How many people get to work for a mere seven and a half minutes a day?" he asked Carol. "If I can't ride and control my horse for seven and a half minutes, I'm a real candyass!"

Irish Cap was ready in the stable, gleaming with good health, in peak condition. Bruce took a critical look at him and turned to Barbara Curtis. "I hope I can make him go as well as you've made him look, Curt," he complimented her.

Riding along the avenue through the great trees of Burghley, Bruce knew that it was one of those days when everything fell into place. The feeling continued as he started to trot around the warm-up arena. "I am sitting on something special, very special," he thought. "He's nice. He's right. I am proud of him."

When the time came for him to perform, Bruce rode smoothly into the competition area. There were a lot of people in the stands, partly because the Queen's horse Columbus, the British favorite, had just finished his test. Most of the people were wearing raincoats and some were eating sandwiches. Irish Cap pricked his ears, drew himself up, and conveyed to Bruce, "Come to the call. Sit up and be somebody. If you can ride, sit on me today." Bruce had a flashback to military school, where his officers had told him, "Stand at brace, Davidson, and stick your chest out."

Riding around the outside of the arena between the audience and the short cropped grass on which he would perform, Bruce lined up carefully so that he would make his entry from the left-hand side to preserve his luck. The starting bell rang. "Judges, you'd better stand up and salute when you see this one coming," thought Bruce, giving Irish Cap the signal to canter.

Irish Cap cantered straight up the centerline and planted his four feet squarely at X, standing like a bronze statue while Bruce removed his black hunt cap to salute the judges. He replaced his cap, picked up the reins, and Irish Cap floated forward in working trot. The movements of the test flowed as smoothly into each other as one stream blends into another, the horse lengthening and shortening his stride at a touch, crossing his legs over in the lateral movements, remaining steady and constant on the bit, making effortless transitions from gait to gait, answering the slightest hint from Bruce. As he made the final turn down the centerline, Bruce smiled happily because this was probably the best test he had ever ridden. He took off his hat with a flourish in the ending salute.

The large, partisan American contingent in the stands exploded into applause as Irish Cap left the scene of his immaculate efforts. The horse acknowledged the noise as his just due, loving the attention. When the scores, which are always given in penalties, were announced, he had gone into the lead with 45.67. Columbus, a difficult horse to ride in the dressage phase because of his nervous temperament, had been temporarily vanquished with a score of 55.67.

Bruce took Irish Cap out behind the dressage arenas to give him one final short gallop to open his lungs before the following day's cross-country. Then he rode him back to the stables, left him with Barbara, and returned to the main arena to watch Mike Plumb ride Good Mixture.

At the end of the day the German team was in the lead with an overall total of 160.33, which was as expected because their traditional strength is in the dressage phase. The Americans, surprisingly, were in second place with 169. The French were third with 172.67, and the British were fourth with 175. One of the very last horses to go, the brilliant Russian stallion Tost, ridden by Vladimir Laniugin, had taken the individual lead from Irish Cap with a score of 42.33. Bruce felt sorry for Irish Cap; he knew that no matter how brilliant the Russian horse had been, it could not have tried harder than his horse had.

V

Waiting is always difficult. Waiting for the beginning of the cross-country is the worst part of any event. Riders worry about the course and how it will jump; they worry about their horses' fitness; they worry about the footing and whether it will hold up under the hooves of sixty or so horses; they worry about their teammates. Tension builds and builds and nerves are stretched so tight that most participants look strained and drawn and one or two giggle when there is nothing to laugh at.

Bruce and Carol went out on the cross-country course early on the Saturday to watch some of the other competitors in action and to try to get a line on how the course was riding. They saw Plain Sailing and Don Sachey, who had had a fall at one of the fences. Plain Sailing's nose was bloody where he had bumped it on a bank, but he galloped on gamely, giving his heart. "That's eventing," Bruce thought. "That's what makes it great: the heart and courage of the great horses."

Walking back to the stables to prepare Irish Cap, Carol noticed something bright and shiny on the grass. Bending down, she picked up a pin. "Look, Bruce," she called. "See a pin and pick it up and all the day you'll have good luck!" She pinned it onto her lapel for safety.

At the stables Barbara was busy screwing studs into Irish Cap's shoes to give him traction on the slippery ground. The big bay was trembling with anticipation, knowing exactly what was ahead and wanting to get out and get going. Bruce pulled on his navy blue turtleneck sweater, checked out his stopwatch, picked up his bat, fixed a piece of tape showing the speeds and distances of the various phases to his wrist, and put on his crash hat with the dark blue cover with red-and-white stripes and "USA" on the front of it. Then he took his saddle over to the scales to weigh in.

The news came in that Denny and Victor Dakin had gone clean. Bruce, as the third rider, had to go clean also to make up for Plain Sailing's fall.

While he waited in the starting box, Irish Cap fretting to be off and bouncing around, Bruce emptied his mind of everything except the ride ahead. As they set off on the first phase of the roads and tracks, a gentle lane that led up to the golf course and the steeplechase, Bruce found that his hands were full of fighting-fit horse — so much so that, winding through the park lined with the centuries-old avenues of lime trees, he was given little time to appreciate his surroundings. Near the end of the first phase he passed Lucinda and Be Fair, who were coming back from their turn around the steeplechase course. Be Fair was also fighting for his head, and the riders exchanged a grin.

"I'm glad to see you're having trouble, too," Lucinda called.

"Yours doesn't look like a piece of cake," Bruce retorted, laughing. "How did it go?" he added.

Lucinda told him that the steeplechase rode well.

Carol was waiting at the steeplechase start in case Bruce needed any help, but since everything seemed in perfect order he just waved to her and stood in the starting box waiting for the signal to go. To his surprise, instead of charging out of the box snatching at the bit, Irish Cap left on a long, relaxed frame, galloping down to the first fence with a reaching stride. At the halfway point Bruce looked at his watch, only to find that he was twenty seconds ahead of time for the first mile of the two-mile course. "My God, Cap," he thought, "how do I slow you down when you aren't even on the bit?" The horse was jumping perfectly, loping along so easily that Bruce could hardly believe his watch was correct, and even though Bruce slowed him to a canter after the last fence he still came in with fifteen seconds in hand.

The two-mile gallop had taken very little out of the big horse; but it had settled him, and Bruce started out on the longer second phase of the roads and tracks with a much more relaxed animal who trotted quietly along until he came close to the start of the cross-country and could see the crowds around the box. Then he began to pull at the reins, because he was anxious.

Bruce dismounted, gave Irish Cap to the team grooms, who took him away to wash him off and check his legs and feet for possible damage, and at once got into a huddle with LeGoff to learn what problems had been encountered by other riders. Any and every little detail could help him now. In a few minutes' time he would be off, and then there would be no further chance to benefit from other people's experiences or to reconsider his own riding plans. LeGoff gave Bruce his last-minute instructions, which were based on what he himself had observed during the day, and ordered him to ride safely because the team needed a clear round. Anxious about the course, thinking of the fences in their proper sequence, Bruce found that half his mind was on the coach's words and the other half on his horse's well-being. He reset his watch, noting as he did so how short a time was left before the start, waved briefly to Carol, who said, "Good luck, Lovey," and walked away to look out on the course.

He remounted and rode into the starting box. From this moment on his mind was empty of anything but his horse and the course.

VI

The starter counted aloud, "Ten, nine, eight, seven, six, five, four, three, two, one — GO!" and Irish Cap leaped out of the box towards the first fence on the course. He took the first three fences with ease, galloping on down towards the Marquess of Exeter's great house. At the fourth fence Bruce jumped the long way around, as ordered, over a single rail as opposed to the big oxer, but the horse jumped so well that he knew

1

1. He has met the correct spot for take-off.

2. This is an excellent sequence. Irish Cap is jumping very well.

3, 4. He is jumping well out beyond this fence, as opposed to dropping too steeply after the rails.

4

5. The rider's upper body must come back in order to support and help rebalance the horse after such a big drop.

6. Notice the strength and support necessary on the stride after landing.

he could have taken the shorter, more difficult way. On down towards the Double Coffin obstacle they went, Irish Cap never breaking his rhythm, looking for his fences, and swinging along with his ears pricked as if he was out for a Sunday afternoon hack. In the surprisingly fluid ease of it all Bruce had time for a mental soliloquy, which went something like this: "I am sitting on a really fancy horse. He's like a schoolteacher who takes a kid by the hand and says, 'Let me teach you to divide.' He's showing me that all those years of training have taught him to think for himself. He *wants* to do this. He's enjoying it."

Vast crowds lining the ropes that cordoned off the course made it seem as if the whole park was filled with people making their way to the most exciting fences and applauding each horse as it galloped by. As he and Cap cruised past the throngs of spectators, snatches of encouraging conversation came to Bruce through the beat of their gallop: "That's Bruce Davidson, the American who did so well at Badminton. He's a lovely rider, isn't he?" Bruce was totally unused to such crowds, but Irish Cap obviously felt that they were all out there just to watch *him*. He pricked his ears as if to say, "*I'll* show you something worth watching!"

At the ninth fence, the little one before the road, Bruce tightened his grip on the reins to slow the horse down. He was still worried that Irish Cap might jump too big and fall. The big bay resented the interference and pulled at the bit. He popped over the fence, dropped down into the road, and galloped on, going so well that Bruce decided to just let him run along on a soft rein and pick his own pace. "I am not going to have to push; I'm not going to have to say whoa. If he settles like this he'll probably make the best time anyway."

Fence 19, the Sunken Road, was a jump very similar to the one at Badminton that had been touch and go for Irish Cap with his big, bold stride. Coming in with particular concentration, the horse took stock of the approach fence, jumped it, took a short stride, and jumped into the road, up onto the bank, and out over the far rails. Bruce grinned and tapped him on the neck. "I'm sorry I doubted you: I apologize. You're a big-time horse now. Come on — run home." Some of the biggest problem fences were ahead, but Bruce knew that his horse was up to any challenge and was not going to make mistakes.

The Waterloo Rails, a nasty sort of fence set on really uneven ground, had caught several horses by surprise because of its big drop down from a difficult takeoff point. Irish Cap jumped out into space and his knees buckled on the landing, but Bruce never thought for a second that his horse would fall. "Any horse can stumble taking a big drop like that, but if it has any class it can recover. Irish Cap, you have class," he thought, holding his head so that Cappy could regain his feet.

The water fence, called the Trout Hatchery, was obscured from distant view by a mass of people who had been drawn to it because of its spectacular falls and eliminations. Irish Cap steadied down the hill, stood back from the rails, landed out in the water, and with no hesitation cantered through the stream and out over the big log on the far side. Applause rang out from the crowd as the American pair disappeared towards the next fence.

And so, in good time, they cleared the final fence, the Raleigh "Chopper" or Guillotine: big, forbidding, and black. Bruce galloped on over the finish line with a grin on his face because his horse, his friend, had just jumped the round of his life. He was exuberant. "I could have been a little old lady out for a Sunday hack," he told Barbara as he dismounted. "I just sat there and let him do it all." Quickly, he undid the girth and took the saddle and stood on the scales to have his weight officially checked. Then he went to cool his horse down before returning to the stables.

Now that the course was behind him Bruce could afford to worry about the fate of the others. Beth Perkins had had a very good ride in spite of her broken foot, and Mike Plumb was to come in with Good Mixture in one of the fastest times of the day, giving the American team three clean rounds. Unfortunately Good Mixture had landed on the back rail of the open water ditch and was a little sore on one leg; and Plain Sailing was suffering with a huge hematoma on his stomach, where he had landed on a fence, and now stood with improvised ice packs strapped to the rapidly swelling bruise. The British team had also finished with three clean rounds. Columbus had taken over individual first place, having had the fastest time on the cross-country course, but there was a rumor that he had hurt a hind leg at the very end of the course.

When the speed and endurance day was finally over the American team had moved into first place in the standings with the scores of their three best rounds adding up to 254 penalty points. The British, with Columbus's fine score to help, were close behind with 292. But if Columbus's leg injury was bad enough to stop him from competing on the final day his score would not apply, in which case the British team total at the end of the cross-country would be 448.20; Chris Collins, the fourth member of their team and for the time being the discard score, had unfortunately had two falls for total penalties of 220.20. No other team was in a position to challenge the Americans.

Bruce went into the competitors' canteen near the stables for coffee and found Jack LeGoff and Mike Plumb already sitting at one of the tables. "Hey, Bruce," called LeGoff, "did you know that you are just twenty-four hundredths of a point in front of Mike?" Bruce had been so elated by the way his horse had performed that he had not even thought about the individual placings. Now he found that he didn't particularly care if Irish Cap won or not because the horse had been everything that he had wanted him to be, and everything that Jack LeGoff had been schooling them both to be for three years. He had galloped in a long frame, using his body as easily as he possibly could, and Bruce had not had to ask him for anything extra from the first fence to the last. He had, moreover, liked what he was doing; and Bruce, listening to the horse's knees snap up at each fence, had enjoyed thinking *Oh, you were so clever right there . . . and that's just what I thought you would do right here.* Bruce had walked the course with thought and had analyzed his horse successfully; and that was what pleased him. Now he felt, "I don't really care how close Good Mixture is because that doesn't pertain to me. My horse is a champion no matter where he finishes."

The euphoria of the American supporters who had cheered their country's magnificent efforts on the course was not reflected in the stables, since even with such a good lead, the team had problems that it might not be able to surmount. Three sound horses were the minimum needed to continue as a team in stadium, and of the four who had gotten round the cross-country course only Irish Cap was in really good shape. Barbara had put poultices on all four of his legs as a precaution, but he was sound and so relaxed that she wondered whether her effort had been necessary. As for the others, Plain Sailing stood in his stall uncomfortably, the ice packs strapped to his belly, Good Mixture had severely bruised a leg, and Victor Dakin had a suspicious-looking tendon. As if these misfortunes were not enough, Caroline Treviranus had fallen at the Waterloo Rails and had broken her collarbone, and Furtive, Beth Perkins's grand old veteran, was quite stiff. The veterinary team, an essential component of all three-day events, worked with ice all night to reduce the swellings and to make the horses more comfortable.

The American stables were not the only ones to have the lights on that night. One of the Russian horses was also having problems, and in the British block the heroic Columbus was uncomfortable from a slipped tendon in his hock.

Nearly all the riders turned up for the traditional cross-country night ball, though for those who were still in contention for the next day's stadium the appearances were mainly brief. Bruce and Carol left early, unable to resist a detour to see if Irish Cap was resting comfortably. Since he was contentedly munching on his hay and ignoring the medical bustle in the stalls around him, Bruce slept soundly.

VII

On the following morning a great crowd of onlookers squashed into the area behind the stables to see the horses paraded for the vital veterinary inspection. The hard night's work by the American veterinary team had been so successful that all of their horses trotted out sound for the official check. Irish Cap, now the overnight individual leader, cheerfully accepted the clapping as his due as he swung down the yard after Bruce. Like the other horses on his team, he had been turned out in immaculate style.

Columbus had been withdrawn officially, and Bruce was sad that he had taken over first place at the expense of injury to one of the really great horses in eventing. Long before he had been selected to train with the U.S. team he had spent time in Ireland as a student at Burton Hall with Sylvia Stanier, and there he had ridden a great gangly young gray horse over gymnastics. That horse had been Columbus.

The morning dragged on for Bruce, who by this time was feeling all the pressures of the competition loading down his shoulders. Walking through the trade stands to the jumping arena to inspect the course for the afternoon competition, he was besieged by friends who said, "Good luck! Win! Win!" As minute crept inexorably after minute he grew more and more nervous, feeling that it would never be time to go and get ready for the final phase. After what felt more like a week than a few hours the crowds began to gather in the arena, waiting for the preliminary jumping competitions to be over, and Bruce and Carol went back to the stables to prepare.

Barbara had braided and polished Irish Cap until his coat reflected every light; his tack was oiled and spotless. Caroline Treviranus was there, her arm in a sling, determined to ride in the parade (though not over the course, which had been forbidden by her doctor). And while the public thronged through the American barn, wanting to see and touch the horses that had gone so well the day before, Irish Cap reveled in the admiration.

Bruce slipped into his team coat, a red one with the blue collar and white facing which are the colors of the United States Equestrian Team, and took his saddle to be weighed out. Before the competition started all the horses and riders had to parade through the stadium. As it happened, the American team was a matched set of big, good-looking bay horses, which made them look more like a team chosen for uniformity of appearance than for quality of performance. They rode into the arena with military precision, grouped tightly in a line of four, the riders in their red coats and black hats smiling at the cheers of the American group in the stands, who were shouting themselves hoarse with patriotic fervor. Walking quietly in front of the Royal Box, they doffed their hats to Prince Philip and the members of the Ground Jury. After this they left the arena for the serious work of warming up for the last test in the three-day competition.

The importance of the coming competition weighed on Bruce, who felt nervous because he was only fractionally in first place and knew that he could not afford a single mistake. Even one time fault would cost Irish Cap the title, and the show jumping phase was the horse's weakest point. He cantered up to a practice fence and Irish Cap hardly left the ground, going instead right through the fence and stumbling to his knees. "Oh God," thought Bruce, "I hope you're not going to do that in the ring, Cap."

Watching the young rider from the edge of the practice ring, Major-General Prior-Palmer, a compassionate and intelligent man who had helped his daughter, Lucinda, through the ordeals of many events, sensed the terrible tension that Bruce was under and came up and put his hand on the young American's knee. "Young man," he said, "remember — we do this for *fun*." "Dammit," thought Bruce, "he's right, you know. And this horse *is* a World Champion whether they give him the ribbon or not; he *is* the best. And that's all this is: a sport. Thank God someone like this man can keep it in the right perspective. Everyone else is saying, 'Win, Bruce, win'; but he's the only one to remind me that I should be a good sport."

The course for the show jumping was big and wide open, with painted fences set on the green turf in the arena and pots of brightly colored flowers to brighten up the massive jumps. The crowds in the stands were packed shoulder to shoulder, many standing on tiptoe for a sight of the final phase of the competition. Irish Cap entered the arena in the American number three team order, and Bruce cantered him up to the judges' stand and took off his cap in salute. The signal to start was sounded. He turned his horse through the starting flags and a great hush fell over the watchers; in the American block hardly anyone took a breath as they followed the round. In perfect style the pair met every fence precisely right, and

Victory gallop at Burghley.

sweeping down to the last combination of jumps they flew on through without a single fault. "He's done it! He's done it!" the well-wishers cheered.

Bruce cantered back to the warm-up area, where he was met by his teammates with handshakes and slaps on the back. "Well done, my friend," LeGoff said exultantly. Irish Cap was indeed the best; he had won the individual gold medal; he was World Champion.

Mike Plumb and Good Mixture also did extremely well, having a clean round with no time faults; but Victor Dakin, showing the results of stress, took three rails down. However, the withdrawal of Columbus gave the Americans a commanding lead for the team title. Of the individuals, Beth Perkins and Furtive finished in sixth place overall, a fine record for the rider with the broken foot.

The awards ceremony had all the elaborate pageantry that the British seem to excel in producing. Led by four trumpeters of the Household Cavalry in their golden uniforms, plus the traditional big skewbald drum

Presentations to the U.S. Team at Burghley: Mike Plumb, Bruce Davidson, Denny Emerson, Don Sachey.

Irish Cap stood for half an hour while Bruce accepted all his awards at Burghley.

horse carrying two immense kettledrums on his sides and guided by reins attached to his rider's feet, the procession of teams filed into the arena. The team honors went to America, with Britain second and Germany third, and the victory gallop around the arena was performed flawlessly, all four American horses moving in cadence, perfectly in line. After the team awards the individual champions rode back in.

Irish Cap walked in flat-footed. He swung his head, looking at the cheering crowd. He was not excited — he was arrogant. There, in honor, were the band, the pipes, the drum horse, but Irish Cap walked in as if to say, "You all didn't believe I would be here did you?" And he stood for almost half an hour with his ears pricked, waiting while the awards were presented. Bruce accepted ribbons, trophies, handshakes, took his hat off, put it back on, took it off again, and Irish Cap just stood there drinking in the applause. He seemed to be thinking, "What took you all so long? Why did we have to go through this whole weekend just to prove ourselves?"

II
The Making of a World Champion

2

The Years Before

About the head of a truly great horse there is an air of freedom unconquerable. The eyes seem to look on heights beyond our gaze. It is the look of a spirit that can soar. It is not confined to horses; even in his pictures you can see it in the eye of the Bonaparte. It is the birthright of eagles.

JOHN TAINTOR FOOTE, *The Look of Eagles*

I

Irish Cap arrived back in the stable yard at Wylye looking as if he had been through a war. Furtive, traveling in the next stall in the horsebox, had attacked him during the journey back from Burghley and had ripped his halter off, smashed his face against the side of the box, and cut his lip. The horse's eye was swollen shut. "*Why?*" demanded Bruce. "Why should he be so unlucky after all he's been through?" Irish Cap, on the contrary, was unperturbed, walking proudly, pleased with himself. The cuts were superficial and in his mind he was well satisfied with his prowess. He knew he had gone well; he took pride in having done so.

Just once in every rider's life there is one horse that means more than all the others put together; one horse that really becomes a friend, really becomes an alter ego. Other horses may be more brilliant and may bring more success, but this one horse remains in the rider's heart forever. Bruce truly loved Irish Cap, not because he had won the World Championships on his back but because he had spent three difficult years of work with the big horse, three long years of hard, painful struggle to learn about three-day eventing.

The American horses were flown back to the United States at the end of September. Bruce and Carol had gone on ahead to their new house in Chester County, just outside Philadelphia, and the new stables at Chesterland Farm were almost completed when Irish Cap and Paddy were driven down from the quarantine station in Clifton, New Jersey, where they had had to stay for twenty-four hours on their return. The homecoming seemed perfect.

Bruce began work with some young horses that he and Carol had bought as event prospects. While he worked he kept a careful eye on Irish Cap, who was turned out each day into the large, green, rolling

OPPOSITE: "Just once in every rider's life there is one horse that means more than all the others put together." Bruce and Irish Cap.

The trust between Irish Cap and Bruce is readily apparent as Bruce trims the horse's whiskers with clippers, using no restraint.

paddocks of Chesterland Farm, and as he watched the big horse a concern grew: something was not right. Irish Cap had always been prone to cough since his wind operation, but now his cough had changed and had a different sound, just as the cough of someone who smokes too much differs from the cough of someone coming down with pneumonia. Irish Cap's cough was now deeper, raspier; it was causing him discomfort.

Bruce rang his veterinarian, J. Allen Leslie, who drove out to the stables with his partner, Matthew Mackay-Smith. They listened to the cough; they listened to Irish Cap's lungs through their stethoscopes, took numerous blood samples, but were unable to come up with a definite diagnosis. Something, they knew, was very wrong, but what was it?

Irish Cap grew progressively worse. Breathing became a visible struggle for him. Soon he could not exert himself without coughing violently. Bruce, who suffers from asthma, watched his horse trying to gulp enough oxygen into his lungs. He was uncomfortably reminded of what he had heard of pneumonia, in which, during the preliminary stages, the victim feels little discomfort: merely a heaviness in the chest. Then the illness strikes and the lungs heave for air, the chest pumps in vain, the mouth gasps for oxygen.

Respirators were fashioned from five-gallon plastic jugs and were fastened to Irish Cap's halter. He stood for hours on crossties in the stable aisle, inhaling various medications prescribed by the veterinarians. Although his condition deteriorated, he appeared normal in every way except that his lungs were desperately infected. It seemed certain that he had picked up an infection in the quarantine station on his journey home, because when he had left England he was fine and when he got home he was not. A report reached Bruce that a horse that occupied the same quarantine stall immediately before Irish Cap had come down with the same ailment. This horse was very ill.

Irish Cap was transferred to the Delaware Equine Center for treatment and further tests. The prognosis was bad: he had developed a cystic condition — small cysts were lodged in the cavities of his lungs, blocking the circulation of air. The blood flow was also greatly reduced, so that the massive doses of antibiotics that were being pumped into him were not able to circulate through his system to fight the infection. The horse remained at the Equine Center for weeks. He was unable to eat and was fed through a stomach tube.

Ill as he was, Irish Cap never lost heart and never gave up. He always had a spark in his eye, and recognized Bruce each time he came to visit, looking at him pleadingly as if to say, "Let me out of here."

Many veterinarians examined him. With only one exception, Allen Leslie, who continued to believe a cure was possible, they recommended that the horse be humanely destroyed.

Bruce called his parents with the bad news. His mother answered the telephone. "Mom, I think Irish Cap is finished," he told her. "The vets have recommended that he be put down. He is terribly ill, but he hasn't given up, Mom."

"Why not take him home and delay any decision?" Mrs. Davidson suggested; and so Irish Cap was taken back to Chesterland, to the home where he was among friends. He remained in his stall, anxious to get out, begging Bruce to let him out again.

II

Bruce's first glimpse of the big horse had been in a stall at the Chagrin Valley Hunt Club in Ohio during a protracted and unsuccessful search for a young horse. Early in 1970 he had been selected to join a training session with the new coach of the United States Equestrian Team's three-day squad, Jack LeGoff, and after the first training session he had been asked to stay on for a second session and then to stay on over the winter. Under the impression that their son would return to college to continue his studies, Bruce's parents preferred to believe that his obsession with horses would soon pass. Bruce was not at all sure that he could persuade his father to let him stay at the team headquarters for the winter, but he did manage to convince him that if he was to be successful at this unfamiliar sport he would need a horse — a young international event prospect — to train.

Jumping at a hunter show on the Polo Field at Myopia, South Hamilton, Massachusetts, long before he thought of trying for the Team. Bruce, age thirteen, on Shirlore.

Bruce, age ten, with his Pony Club horse and favorite hunter, Cecil.

Bruce had one ally in his corner: his grandmother. As a small boy Bruce and his grandfather, a big, tough man, had been the greatest of friends. The man had shared his love of animals, and especially of horses, with his grandson, and the two had learned to respect and love each other. After his grandfather's death Bruce's grandmother had encouraged the young boy in his interest, seeing a reflected love coming from her husband.

When he had first tried out for selection to the team, Bruce had asked Bertalan de Nemethy, the Hungarian coach of the U.S. Equestrian Team jumping squad, for advice on places to go and train for the summer. De Nemethy suggested Burton Hall in Ireland, and Bruce spent one summer there. Just before he went up to Gladstone to train with LeGoff, de Nemethy introduced the young rider to his friend Gabor Foltenyi, who is well known for his eye for good horses. Now that Bruce was about to embark on a search for a horse, he called on Gabor for help. They lined up over three hundred prospects, and, as most of these were stabled in the Philadelphia area, Gabor flew to Philadelphia to meet Bruce. They drove mile after mile and looked at horse after horse. All were rejected by Bruce's adviser, and by the time they had searched for an entire week Bruce was beginning to lose hope of finding a horse that he both wanted and could afford on his limited pocketbook. While Mr. Davidson had given his permission to search for a horse, he had made it perfectly clear that Bruce did not have unlimited funds to spend.

At the end of the week Bruce and Gabor drove dejectedly back to Philadelphia to spend the last night before returning home. "There *is* one more horse we could look at," Gabor said. "He's at the Chagrin Valley Hunt Club in Ohio, and belongs to Howard Lewis. He's six years old, sixteen-one hands, and is meant to be a lovely mover; but I hear he has big ankles, so he may not be suitable." At this point Ohio seemed as remote as Ireland to Bruce, but he thought that perhaps he should go there just in case this horse might be the very one he wanted. After all, everything else had failed, so there didn't seem much to lose except the fare.

They flew to Ohio and drove out to the Hunt Club. The horse was indeed a nice mover and was also available at a reasonable price, but Gabor felt that he would not stand up to the rigors of eventing. Bitterly disappointed, Bruce wandered down the stables, waiting for Gabor to change out of his riding clothes.

In the stall next to the horse they had just rejected stood a big bay gelding. Bruce leaned over the door of the stall and came face to face with a big horse who looked him straight in the eye. Struck by the horse's size and by the sheer intelligence in its big brown eyes, feeling a sense of recognition, Bruce went in search of Gabor.

"Can we just have a look at that one over there?" he asked.

Gabor glanced over quickly. "No. He's too big."

"I think we *should* look at him," begged Bruce.

Mr. Lewis led the horse out of the stall into the yard. "Wow!" Gabor said. "What *is* this horse? He looks nice out of his stall." He changed back into his riding breeches and got on the big gelding. The horse was completely green, awkward and gangling in his movements, but he had

Irish Cap in 1970.

that indefinable look of quality that knowledgeable horsemen recognize. Bruce thought he looked wonderful (at that stage in his life he thought almost any horse looked wonderful), but he had also had that private moment of recognition with the horse. He was not looking for a horse to build a reputation on; he was looking for a horse he wanted, a horse to learn to ride on, not just a good-looking, pretty horse.

"Plenty of horses, and plenty of people for that matter, are pretty to look at," he said later, "but that doesn't mean you want to spend your life with them. Anyone can dissect somebody and say, 'You're too tall; you have too big a waist; you have too big a nose; you have buck teeth; I don't like your eyebrows; I don't like the way you cut your hair.' It isn't important — those are cosmetics and you don't want to spend your life at a cosmetic counter, you want to spend your life with real people. The same is true of horses. You want to spend your life with a horse you *like*."

The bay was certainly not a cosmetic horse. He had lots of bone and a roman nose, but he had presence. Bruce had a strong feeling that this was perhaps the horse he had been searching for all along, a horse that would help him achieve his goal, a horse with potential for learning, and above all a horse he could like.

There was one problem: the horse cost more than Bruce's father's budget had allowed for. Bruce tried to talk Mr. Lewis down in price, but to no avail, though Mr. Lewis did agree to ship the horse up to the team headquarters in Gladstone so that LeGoff could see him and he could be vetted for soundness. He told Bruce he could have the horse at Gladstone for twenty-four hours in which to make up his mind.

When the horse arrived at the team headquarters LeGoff took an instant liking to him. "He certainly is a big horse, my friend," he told Bruce, watching the great gelding walk around the stable yard. "Let's see what he can do."

Knowing how very green the horse really was, Bruce was too scared to tell his coach the truth: the horse had only been under saddle for two weeks and could hardly be expected to display much in the way of ability. He moved on the flat like a hackney pony, his knees snapping up and his stride jerky.

"Let's see if he can jump," said LeGoff. "Jump this little fence first."

With his heart in his mouth Bruce cantered down to a small hogsback and the horse lurched over it.

"That's not very impressive," LeGoff said. "Do it again."

The second attempt was very impressive indeed.

Bruce on the recently purchased Irish Cap not being able to put the horse between his hand and leg.

"All right — let's see what he does over this ditch," ordered LeGoff.

The horse cantered down to the ditch and made a gigantic leap in the air over it. Bert de Nemethy, who had come out to watch this new prospect, was astonished. "My God! " he exclaimed. "Gabor is *my* friend. Why does he not get *me* a horse like this? "

"Try him over water, Bruce," LeGoff suggested; so Bruce rode the horse down to the water jump, where he plunged in and considered trying to jump over the high wall on the other side.

"I like him," said LeGoff. "Buy him."

III

Falling more and more in love with the horse, Bruce called at once for the veterinarian, who came out with his X-ray unit and subjected the animal to a thorough three-hour examination. On the following day he telephoned with bad news, reporting that the horse had a fracture in one of his front feet. Hopelessly disappointed, Bruce put the horse on a van and sent him back to Ohio.

Sensing the young rider's misery, LeGoff invited him to dinner and told him many stories of horses that had failed a veterinary examination but had turned out to be perfectly sound. He said that X-rays were not always dependable. Bruce called his family to explain and to suggest that perhaps they should get a second opinion, considering that LeGoff had said that this was one of the most exceptional young horses he had ever seen in his life. After that he rang Mr. Lewis, which took courage. It is not easy to ask for a second look at a horse that one has just rejected. "The horse hasn't even arrived back here in Ohio," he was told; but after a long conversation Mr. Lewis agreed to keep the horse for seven days and then to ship him back, at Bruce's expense, to the Veterinary School at New Bolton, Pennsylvania, for exhaustive tests. At New Bolton, Dr. Jenny, one of the teaching staff, decided that the original diagnosis had been mistaken and that the horse had no fracture.

Bruce telephoned his family again, reporting that although the horse had been rejected by the first vet, there seemed, after all, to be nothing wrong with him. "This is *the* horse," he said fervently: *his* horse. There was already a bond between them, a recognition of each other. Listening to the excited voice on the other end of the telephone, Bruce's family agreed to buy him the horse, and on September 1, 1970, Irish Cap became the proud possession of Bruce Davidson. No bells rang, no fireworks exploded; the world went on, unnoticing, but Bruce was changed inside. His family had made it possible for him to realize his lifelong ambition. A whole new life was about to begin.

IV

Now that he had his horse, Bruce found to his dismay that he couldn't ride one side of him. Big, awkward, barely broken to the saddle, the horse went charging around with his head in the air, his movements spastic, under little control. Bruce wondered if he would ever be able to ride well enough to cope with all the problems. LeGoff, meanwhile, was

Jack LeGoff.

LEFT: The coach enjoyed his own career in international competition. He competed for France in the Rome Olympic Games in 1960 on Image.

scathing. He himself could get on and make the horse do any number of things while Bruce watched from the side, but, try as he might, Bruce could not even get the horse to lower his nose, flex his neck, and come onto the bit.

The other candidates at the training sessions were merciless. "Hey, Davidson," they jeered at him, "why did you go and buy a big, green horse like that? You're crazy. You'll never make the team that way." But Bruce wasn't interested in making the team. He wanted only to learn to ride, and riding on an Olympic team was incidental to his desire to ride horses as well as he could. He watched LeGoff on horseback with reverence, wondering if he would ever be able to present a horse as the coach could. In the depth, the strength, the finesse, and the presence he produced with each horse he mounted, there was an image that the young rider vowed somehow to re-create for himself. To this day, Bruce enjoys watching his teacher ride a horse.

Learning to ride is somewhat the same as learning to write. The first letters of a child are clumsy, straggling capitals that stray around the paper. The small fingers on the pencil struggle to contain the As, Bs, and Cs. Similarly, the beginning rider tugs on the reins, struggles with the rising trot, loses balance as the horse moves forward, and kicks away with legs flapping on the horse's sides. Gradually the child begins to write in large, clear script, joining the letters for a better flow; the rider finds balance, learns to coordinate hands and legs, and finds that moving with the horse is not as impossible as it seemed at first, and that a glimmer of the correct position makes it easy to influence the horse. Handwriting then takes on individual characteristics, all distinctive to the particular hand and eye, and at a similar stage the rider learns to travel at speed, to jump, to make the horse move laterally, and to follow the movements in sequence. Most writers and most riders stop here, content with having mastered the basic requirements; but a few, not satisfied, pursue their art to its limit, refining their skills until the hand produces the flawless copperplate of the master calligrapher, and the rider produces the finely trained horse that reaches the top in any of the disciplines of equitation.

Jack LeGoff came from the famous French cavalry school at Saumur, where he had learned his craft from a tradition of teaching evolved over four centuries. He was steeped in the military routine, he was new to America (he spoke only marginal English), and he was under extreme pressure to produce an Olympic team for the games to be held in Munich in 1972. He set about this in the only way he knew how: he treated the young prospective riders as raw recruits, putting them through the cavalry version of basic training or boot camp.

In a very short space of time, Bruce and the other young riders learned to speak only when spoken to. They never questioned, they got out of the way in the halls, never went upstairs ahead of LeGoff, and felt completely without rank in his presence. This was alien to all the traditionally independent American riders except Bruce, who had attended a military prep school, McDonough, and had learned early on to say, "Yes sir! No sir! No excuse, sir!" For him the discipline was perfectly normal.

All the riders, male and female alike, were expected to look after their own horses, to feed and groom them, to muck out the stables, and to do all the rest of the physical labor connected with the upkeep of a competition horse. They were under orders to keep their weight down and to jog a certain number of miles per week to get themselves as fit as their horses.

Before a rider can be truly effective the basic position in the saddle has to be thoroughly established. The human body must fit into the horse, becoming part of the animal and moving in complete balance no matter what the speed or what the effort the horse is making. There is only one way to achieve this, and it is a painful one — riding for hours without stirrups to develop the correct muscles. Training sessions with LeGoff were grueling, the riders spending five hours or more per day on a horse, drilling in line, riding either without stirrups or with stirrups tied to the saddle to stabilize the leg position. They each had a pair of what became known as "bloody breeches," stained red where contact had chafed the skin. They were put on horses with no reins on the bridle and no stirrups on the saddle and were sent around the indoor school by people stationed at each end with the lunge whips. The horses jumped over big fences set at odd distances, and the riders had to learn to absorb the shock of the jump through their backs. They were sent down grids with their faces turned towards the coach so that they could not see what lay ahead or when the horse would jump.

Each day they sat down for a lecture on the theory of riding and training. Bruce, anxious to show his enthusiasm, sat in the front row, watching the circles being drawn on the blackboard until his eyelids

Bruce riding at the Gladstone training sessions, age nineteen.

Gaining vital experience, Bruce rides Bold Lur, a USET horse, over the cross-country course at Fair Hill 1970.

Story Jenks on a young horse at the new water jump at Gladstone, New Jersey.

"This was a complex water jump beginning with a 3'3" vertical fence with a drop into water, followed by two strides in the water out onto an island bank of 24 feet, back down into water with one full stride in the water, and then out over another vertical fence.

"This is an example of my concern that too much is being made of water fences. This is a combination of five elements involving water and has the added difficulty of jumping from the light into darkness. And this is a fence on a Preliminary course!"

3, 4. As he jumps he turns sharp left. In fact, the moment he hits the water he turns parallel to the fence, making it extremely difficult for the rider to stay on.

5. As he turns he loses footing with his hindquarters, making it even more difficult to stay on.

6, 7, 8, 9. The determination of the rider pays off as he begins to recover, and although the horse goes out at the side of the splash he is immediately brought back in.

2

1. As the horse is preparing to leave at the point of take-off he is looking very hard but being encouraged strongly by a good rider. Already the horse is thinking about running out to the left.

2. As he jumps into the water he is still only going because of the strong encouragement of the rider. The horse looks very hesitant about getting his feet wet.

4   **5**

8   **9**

Continued overleaf.

10

10, 11, 12, 13, 14. Story Jenks rides strongly through the remaining elements of the combination.

11

12

13

14

drooped and his head nodded and he fell fast asleep. A roar from LeGoff brought him back to wakefulness, only to drop off again. As long as he stayed on his feet he was fine and could go all day, but as soon as he took his feet off the floor sleep took him like an exhausted child. LeGoff was not amused by this proclivity.

V

Bruce was shy to the point of agony, and he knew none of the other team candidates. At lunchtime he would sit in the stables with his one friend, Irish Cap, watching the horses eating, enjoying the sounds of the stable. Sometimes he wondered if he was doing the right thing: he knew he was passive as a rider, and that he had only just begun to realize how much knowledge he lacked, but even so he had to ask himself if it was necessary for his coach to be so harsh.

"I can stick it out because I want to be here," he thought. "O.K.: I'll push myself every bit as hard as he wants and I'll do everything he says; but why does he have to insult me and belittle me? I'm left at night without even myself as a friend. If I go on taking this abuse I'm not sure I'll like myself anymore."

It was a time when he had reached a plateau, and he had to be pushed on so that he could progress. Without ever saying so, LeGoff understood just how to turn the quiet, shy boy into a horseman capable of competing against the world's best riders in tough international competitions where any weakness becomes a major fault.

After the initial training sessions the other riders left and Bruce was the only occupant of the quarters above the stables. Autumn drew on into a long, cold, raw winter, and he felt more and more alone. At night, when he finished up in the stables, he would look around at the horses bedded down in the deep golden straw, eating their grain and walking over to munch on the sweet-smelling hay. It was, for him, the best time of all: the horses moving in their stalls, being content.

He was riding team horses as well as Irish Cap. Plain Sailing, an old campaigner, taught him the feeling of many of the dressage movements, and he learned to cope with difficult horses such as Bold Lur, who was temperamental and scatterbrained. He rode Fairystone, a big gray horse who was stiff and somewhat arthritic. He learned how to bend horses correctly, to make them step with their hind legs under the mass of the weight, to lighten them; and all the time he tried his best to transfer what he was learning to Irish Cap.

It took him nine months to put Irish Cap onto the bit, since LeGoff would not countenance any shortcuts, insisting that the young rider learn the right way to produce a horse. It was a time of learning for both of them. Irish Cap was a horse before his time. Bruce was not able to develop his potential as quickly as he would have liked, because he himself was essentially unschooled, but the long, slow process of learning to ride Irish Cap and to train him taught Bruce well and was the making of him as a rider. Irish Cap was trained according to principles laid down in the basic manuals which had been added to through four centuries of experience. Each step arose from the previous one, and each had to be

Irish Cap and Bruce in the early days of competition.

perfected before moving up. The training of Irish Cap took three years.

The pressures of that first winter nearly cracked Bruce's resolve. On New Year's Eve, 1970, he got up at 4 A.M., spent a routine day, and finished up his chores at 7:30 P.M. After looking around the stables he said goodnight to Irish Cap, turned out the lights, and climbed the steps to his lonely room above. No one else lived there: he was the only human in the building. He sat on his bed and listened to the silence of his own company.

"It's New Year's Eve," he thought. "It's my twenty-first birthday, and here I am. This is meant to be a big deal. I can drink now. I am supposed to *do* something." He felt like crying. "You can't cry," he told himself. "You are twenty-one years old and it's time you had your own life. I guess my own life goes to bed at eight P.M. After all, it's my choice to be here." He warmed up his TV dinner and went to bed, feeling very sorry for himself. Ailsa and Denny Crawford, friends who lived just down the road from the stables, gave him a Jack Russell terrier puppy to cheer him up.

VI

No winter lasts forever. The spring sun warmed the ground, the frosts thawed, the trees were touched with a tinge of green, and Bruce found that the agonizing hours in the saddle had given him a new balance on a horse. He could feel the horse's movements and could anticipate the next step, beginning to be part of the horse instead of a mere appendage stuck on top. Since Irish Cap had learned to come onto the bit, Bruce found that he was now expected to teach the horse to stretch. Riding is like that; one achievement opens the way to the next challenge.

In addition to his lessons with LeGoff, Bruce spent any spare time watching the jumping riders working with Bert de Nemethy. He was given the chance to ride some of the show jumping team horses, and he learned new skills jumping over big stadium fences of five feet and more. He found that the longer he was able to take the rigorous training, the more he was offered some extracurricular things to do for fun. Life became bearable. He began to compete. His heart still lay with Irish Cap, and their mutual learning process had two years yet to run.

3

The Four-Year Plan

. . . he grew into his seat
And to such wondrous doing brought his horse
As he had been incorps'd and demi-natured
With the brave beast

SHAKESPEARE, *Hamlet*

I

Marie Joseph Paul Yves Roch Gilbert du Motier, Marquis de Lafayette, sailed from France on April 25, 1777, aboard the ship *La Victoire* to help America in its fight against British domination. The American army, frantic with need for trained officers who could shape its ragtag conglomeration of volunteers into a force able to fight against the European regulars, made the experienced marquis a major general on arrival. Lafayette was a man of great authority. On an expedition to the northernmost states he so impressed the Oneida Indians that they switched their allegiance from the British to the American cause (possibly also influenced by the gold French coins that Lafayette so generously handed out) and gave their new friend the Indian name Kayewha, meaning "fearsome horseman."

On March 1, 1970, another Frenchman came to the aid of America — this time by jumbo jet to New York's J.F.K. Airport — bringing much-needed expertise to the United States Equestrian Team's losing battle against the worldwide British domination of the three-day event. Jack Louis Joseph LeGoff had a width of knowledge far beyond that of any trainer in America. He had ridden with the famous Cadre Noir, the Black Squadron of the French cavalry which demonstrates all the elegant, highly refined movements of the Haute Ecôle, the pinnacle of dressage riding. He had also raced steeplechasers over the tough European circuits, and had been three-day champion of France in 1956 and 1963. He had ridden on the bronze-medal-winning French three-day team at the Rome Olympics, and had coached the French three-day team for the Mexico Olympics, where his student J. J. Guyon won the individual gold medal; and if these qualifications were not enough to impress the three-day world wherever his shadow fell across it, he had for many years been the trainer at Saumur, the tough French cavalry academy where only the best can ever hold the post.

OPPOSITE: Bea Perkins on County Frost receives last-minute directions before the stadium jumping.

Whitney Stone, a persuasive ambassador for the U.S. Equestrian Team, had flown to Paris hoping to persuade this superman to export his knowledge to the American side. The interview took place in a hotel room, and since Whitney Stone spoke no French and LeGoff spoke only a minimum of English, LeGoff's wife, Madeleine, sat between the two, laboriously translating offer and counteroffer. The bargaining lasted all day. As the light faded westwards out of the Paris sky an agreement was made that was to bring about a revolution in American eventing; a second American revolution in a tinier, more specialized world, a contest once more won with the help of a Frenchman who knew how to slice the British in their shins. The Oneidas would have recognized LeGoff as Kayewha reincarnated.

Lafayette told Washington, "It is to learn and not to teach that I come hither," but LeGoff made it plain from the start that he had come to teach. He intended to teach riders to ride, and to teach them to train their horses, and to teach America what this sport was all about. He did not intend to allow a second to slip by that could profitably be used.

The headquarters of the U.S. three-day team, since moved to Massachusetts, were at the time located with the other branches of the U.S. Equestrian Team at Gladstone, New Jersey. The facility is buried in deep woods, hidden from view until one reaches the top of a long drive that twists and turns through pine trees, ending in a square courtyard in front of the main building. A vast stable block with steeply pitched, dark-brown-tiled roofs, its gables outlined in aquamarine trim, houses the team horses in enormous loose boxes of dark, polished wood. Each stall is topped by aquamarine bars which are crowned by large brass knobs kept sparkling with gallons of Brasso. The floors of the stalls are of stone and the aisleways are made of yellow stable brick. The stalls are built on two levels: the bigger upper level, which is on the approach side, also contains the team office rooms, while the floor below looks out onto a sharp drop in the ground, facing away from the entrance, which is set higher up on the hill. In the middle of the upper floor the walls of the rotunda shine with plaques won at international competitions, and upstairs, leading off the rotunda, is the official USET trophy room, where glass-fronted cabinets protect the silver trophies won by American teams in World and Olympic competitions. From the trophy room, French doors open onto a terrace overlooking the large sand arena, curtained by a gray stone wall, that is used for practice sessions, for demonstrations, and for occasional competitions. On the lower level is the indoor riding ring, Nautical Hall, named after the famous palomino show jumper who was called "the horse with the flying tail."

Impressed though he was with the magnificent facilities for the horses, LeGoff could not be satisfied until he had seen the surrounding countryside. A three-day horse needs lots of room for its training, and although the rolling countryside was adequate, it was not ideal because too much of the land had been built on. Feeling slightly uneasy, but still with the stirrings of freedom in his heart, he went down into the stables to look at the horses themselves; and this time he was not impressed. There were three horses, all of them old campaigners, all with problems of one sort or another, and all with a good bit of age on them. They were not, he thought, a promising nucleus for a championship team.

Madeline LeGoff walks the cross-country course with her husband.

All good revolutions need a plan, and all good plans have set goals. LeGoff's immediate goal was to produce a team for the 1972 Olympic Games, which lay only two years ahead — not, on the face of it, a promising prospect with three old horses, some self-taught riders, and several young, green hopefuls. His long-range plan was to develop a system to bring along young riders and potential international horses to create a pool of talent for international competition.

His search for talent began at once. A list of candidates had been drawn up by Bert de Nemethy, who had traveled around the country looking for possible jumping riders. Among the names on his list was that of Bruce Davidson. Very few of the riders on the list had had any real experience in three-day events; most had been spotted in the hunt field or on the show circuit. Bruce had perhaps the least experience of the lot. He was essentially unschooled in any of the basic principles of riding — raw material ready to be molded into a finished product.

LeGoff started on his training program right away. He took the young

Officials in Kentucky are amused to watch LeGoff sweeping up after one of his horses at the veterinary inspection.

riders and immersed them in a stream of work. He insisted that each detail be perfect, he nagged at them, he shook their bad habits out of them, he restructured their position on a horse, he taught them to think like a horse and to anticipate every move. No one in America had ever spent so much time on the basics before; instead, the riders had gone out Yankee fashion and had simply done what was needed (if they could). Riding horses without stirrups for hours on end was too serious a come-down for many of the established riders, who had grounds for thinking that they knew how to ride, and so LeGoff's eventual nucleus was drawn from the young, green hopefuls who had no illusions about their abilities.

LeGoff's system led off with giving the riders the basic skills and then teaching them how to use these skills. He was a hard taskmaster. He drilled his pupils incessantly, insisting on perfection, ranting and raving when they failed to satisfy him — which was constantly — and driving them without mercy. He masterminded every step along the way, orchestrating the development of style. No detail was too small to be overlooked, no incident went unnoticed, and nothing short of perfection would fulfill him. It was perhaps as well for the riders that LeGoff arrived in America speaking practically no English — the stream of exasperated words that were hurled at them as they struggled to improve were spoken in a language that they did not understand.

LeGoff is a tall man, very elegant and erect. His face has the roseate glow of an outdoorsman and his blue eyes can twinkle with amusement or frost into slits of ice with awful disapproval. His teaching is physical as well as verbal. He uses his whole body in his coaching sessions, showing each rider the movement he needs to make; he also waves his arms with Gallic abandon to emphasize a point, or stamps his foot, or covers his eyes in disgust.

LeGoff leaves nothing to chance. Each of his riders receives intense individual instructions in competition. Here he counsels Tad Coffin in preparation for his ride on Dixie Grey in Kentucky 1979.

A coach must be many things: teacher, taskmaster, example, friend; but above all he must be a shrewd psychologist. He must know when to push, when to cajole, when to scold, when to shout, and when to praise. Each rider is an individual. Some, such as Bruce, need to be goaded into action and others need to be coaxed, though all must learn to take constant pressure if they are to succeed in international competition. A riding coach has a double burden, having to deal not only with the individual rider but also with each individual horse. And, like each rider, each horse requires a different approach. Some horses need to be soothed, some to be driven, some to be commanded; each has a temper and a rhythm of its own, and it is the job of the riding coach to fit horse and human together, acting very much like the old-fashioned marriage broker. Certain partnerships are naturals while others are disasters; not every rider suits every horse. LeGoff's extraordinary knowledge both of horses and of people enables him to put the right rider on the right horse and to produce the winning combinations.

In preparation for the 1972 Olympics the American horses had to be shipped to Europe in the early spring in order to beat a strict quarantine imposed because of an outbreak of infectious equine anemia on the North American continent. In addition to the most likely team candidates, LeGoff took several young horses and riders with him to continue their education at their temporary base in England. Among these were Bruce Davidson and Irish Cap.

By this time Bruce was growing confident in his riding, having won the Canadian Championships in the previous fall on Plain Sailing, one of the great old campaigners of the USET, and he was chafing under the yoke of the coach. He thought he could do well enough without constant supervision. LeGoff sensed his pupil's impatience and felt a twinge of

uneasy triumph, knowing that the more talent a rider has the more difficult it is to coach him. Anyone who has studied the art of riding has found it to be akin to mountain climbing; there are long, steep slopes to climb to reach a plateau. The plateau invariably leads to another slope, then another plateau, and so it goes. At the lip of each successive plateau a great feeling of accomplishment is felt as the rider thinks, "Aha! *Now* I know." It takes a while to realize that this is only another beginning and that the slopes and the plateaus are infinite.

At the competition at Tidworth, one of the pre-Olympic British trials which LeGoff had chosen to test his riders out, Bruce was to ride Irish Cap in one section and Bold Lur, a team horse, in another. LeGoff announced that he would not help Bruce at all in the warm-up area, which elated the young rider because by then he was beginning to think that he would not even be allowed to blow his nose by himself. Irish Cap won his section easily, and Bruce changed his saddle onto Bold Lur, thinking to himself, "It's about time I did this alone. Thank goodness that I can at last get on with it in my own way."

As he got into the warm-up area he realized that it was not going to be so easy. Bold Lur, a difficult, scatterbrained horse, temperamental and nervous, grew more and more tense under Bruce's hand.

"Somebody should be out here telling me to do this and to do that," Bruce thought. "What do I *do* with this horse? He's not listening to me."

The horse got worse, and Bruce, losing control of his temper, kicked him hard. Bold Lur exploded, and the dressage test was a disaster. The coach had made his point: Bruce was not ready to be on his own. In the local newspaper the next day the headline read, *Davidson Leads One Section — Is Bottom in the Other.*

"You see," LeGoff said. "You *see*! I leave you alone and you go and lose your temper and punish the horse with your legs. You must learn to take the pressure."

The point had been made the hard way.

II

After the Olympic Games in Munich, where the Americans won the team silver medal, LeGoff began at once to work with new horses and riders who showed talent. He set up his four-year plan. Based on the Olympic cycle, the plan makes use of the post-Olympic year to seek out promising riders. LeGoff tours the country, observing riders at competitions which are designated as selection trials, and those who catch his eye are invited to a training session at the team headquarters, now in South Hamilton, Massachusetts. While explaining that this is meant as a reward for good performance, LeGoff in reality is making use of the chance to investigate each rider's potential. Candidates are subjected to a vigorous three weeks to see how they react. They learn much in a short time — mainly how little they really know — and those who stand out from the crowd are asked to train with LeGoff for about nine months of each year until the next Olympic Games is reached.

Unfortunately there is only room for four candidates at a time at the team headquarters, so LeGoff spends many weeks in weeding out the

OPPOSITE: Bruce gives intense instructions to a pupil, reflecting the dedication he learned from his own teacher, LeGoff. Recuperating from a badly smashed foot, he lays his crutches aside to make a point more emphatically.

Bruce rides Paddy in front of the new three-day team headquarters in South Hamilton, Massachusetts.

four with the most potential. As always, his selections are made with his peculiar understanding of what it takes to make an international star: there are many competent riders who lack that extra quality, that core of steel, that makes them true international competitors.

"The competitive spirit has to be *born* in a rider," he explains. "You cannot put it there if it is not there to start with."

He considers a rider's background carefully. If two candidates have equal ability but one has had years of coaching while the other is self-made, LeGoff will prefer the latter because he has more potential for improving with good coaching.

Above all, LeGoff insists that a candidate must be organized, able to think and to understand, because without a disciplined mind a rider will not succeed in three-day eventing. Finally, the rider must take pressure from the coach, day in and day out. Otherwise, when it comes down to the all-important competition and the rider goes out on his horse in front of fifty thousand pairs of eyes and the pressure hangs like a leaden weight, what will happen?

LeGoff is a classic example of a martinet; moreover, hard as he is on all his riders, there is always one unlucky character on whom he is especially hard. It has become a standard joke among team members, who are gathered for intensive discipline six weeks ahead of any competition, that one of them will be selected to sweat in the steam of the coach's relentless pressure. "Who's going to catch it this time?" they ask each other, knowing that the scapegoat will do nothing right no matter how obediently he works. Bruce played the victim as a young rider; but since the reassuring American supreme performance at Montreal in 1976, which proved beyond question that earlier successes could not have been due to freak luck, he has noticed a softening in his coach's manner.

"Jack now says that his ultimate goal is to train the whole team and never have a row and never get mad with anyone," he says. "And that's a big step that would be very hard for him.

"When he first came he spoke very little English. Also he's a very sensitive guy, and when we were all together I often watched him and had a feeling that when we told a joke and laughed he wondered whether we were laughing at him. And that must be a very hard situation to be in when you don't know the language well enough to follow it, the conversation is too fast for you, yet you hear your name intermittently. We were laughing about incidents in the day, but I can see how it could be very easy to wonder if people were making fun of you."

This strong-willed man who pushes his riders to their limits in practice is the man they rely on entirely in competition, where LeGoff takes charge of every move. He makes it possible for the riders to concentrate entirely on their own tasks. He is the source of strength, giving full confidence to the riders because they know at all times that he is there in charge, neglecting no detail, no observation that could help. He walks the cross-country course with them and counsels each individual rider on what to expect from each individual horse. He is omnipresent — rider, groom, farrier, veterinarian, and course observer can count on him to know their jobs, and they trust him implicitly.

III

Bruce Davidson, the first product of LeGoff's magnificent system, won the individual World Championships in 1974 and again in 1978. The second product, Tad Coffin, won the individual gold medal at the Pan American Games in 1975 and followed it up with the individual gold medal at the Olympic Games in Montreal in 1976. No other country has set up such a controlled program, and were it not for the international thrashings meted out by LeGoff, no such program would have evolved because the European nations have a natural selection system in their well-established calendar of events.

England, for example, chooses its international short list on the basis of riders' performances all over Europe during the preceding fall. The candidates are screened at Badminton in April, after which a provisional short list is announced, followed by tryouts at one or another of the many home events available in midsummer. America is still far behind in offering three-day events on a regular basis, and it is hard for riders to gain much-needed international experience with no international competition to speak of on the western side of the Atlantic.

Apart from Badminton, England's varied calendar includes the internationally flavored Burghley in the autumn, which gives riders and horses a chance to sharpen their skills at both ends of the season. The British riders excel at galloping and jumping across country and until recently have paid little attention to the dressage phase, though now that other nations have become equally adept at speed and endurance, the dressage scores have more influence on the final result. In consequence, more and more British riders are going over to the Continent to polish their dres-

Judy Bradwell (GB) on Castlewellan through the water at Badminton 1979.

"Fortunes can change dramatically in any three-day competition. Judy Bradwell won the dressage phase on Castlewellan, but this unfortunate stop on the cross-country course cost them the prize.

"This water complex is another example of the trend nowadays of making complicated combinations involving water."

1. As the horse jumps through the bounce he seems to drift to the right.

1

4  **5**

7  **8**

2 **3**

6

4, 5, 6. Upon landing in the water he has to make a sharp turn to the left which upsets his concentration.

7. At this stage the horse seems to be unsure as to where he is supposed to go and is carrying his head too high to see the next element.

8, 9, 10. He meets the bank up out of the water on a very long stride, making a tremendous effort, and the rider is caught behind the motion as he lands on top.

9 **10**

Continued overleaf.

14, 15, 16, 17, 18. On the second try all goes well and Castlewellan makes a big leap out.

11, 12, 13. Neither horse nor rider seems organized as to what happens next, resulting in a refusal at the last element.

2

5   **4**

Jane Holderness–Roddam (GB) on Warrior at the Footbridge, Badminton 1979.

1

1. This was an option fence, and the rider has chosen to take the most direct route across the middle. It was the biggest effort but the fastest way.

2. The horse has made a good take-off.

3

3. Over the top of the fence the tremendous thrust of the take-off has forced the rider behind the motion in midair.

4. She has allowed the reins to slip but does not lose the contact.

5. As a result, when the horse pecks on the landing after the gigantic leap, she is secure in the saddle and ready to assist him in the following stride.

Lucinda Prior-Palmer (GB) riding Killaire through the Sunken Footpath, Badminton 1979.

"This is a difficult combination with a vertical fence followed by a drop and a ditch beyond. The horses tend to look down into the ditch and pay less attention to the vertical."

1. The horse is jumping nicely and the rider is secure in the saddle and ready to assist at any moment.

2. As the horse goes down the slope the rider is allowing it to use its head and neck to see the ditch and find the footing, yet she keeps her weight back and is not pulled forward.

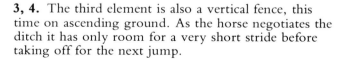

3, 4. The third element is also a vertical fence, this time on ascending ground. As the horse negotiates the ditch it has only room for a very short stride before taking off for the next jump.

5. The rider lets her reins remain too long but compensates by taking her arms back behind her body to maintain the necessary contact.

6, 7. Safely over and the rider has to shorten her reins again in order to gallop on towards the next fence.

2

4

6 **7**

sage in the traditional German schools, since no central training program is available at home. And because the team trainer only comes into action after the final short list has been drawn up, he has little chance to work effectively if his riders and horses are not fit and polished when they arrive with him.

The German riders, who have a well-established training center at Warendorf with resident trainers supported by the state, can avail themselves at any time of the best help in the country. But German horses tend to be big and heavy. Although they are dominant in the dressage ring, they are not as fast across country as their English and American Thoroughbred rivals. When one of these heavy horses opens up its stride, thundering along like a medieval warhorse, it goes *pa-dum, pa-dum, pa-dum,* like a big bass drum; while the longer-reaching stride of the Thoroughbred eases past, *tt-ttut, tt-ttut, tt-ttut,* like a snare drum, kicking across the ground with the least of effort.

The Irish, more horse-minded as a nation than any other, have the advantage of producing the best horses in the world on their breeding farms. Choose a team horse at random from any country and you will be more than likely to come up with an Irish-bred. They have a first-class coach in Jock Ferrie, but there is no systematic program and their riders have to develop themselves to a great extent.

Russian training methods and systems are unkown, except in Russia. There is a large training establishment outside Moscow, and Russian teams make sporadic excursions into the eventing world and vanish again behind the Iron Curtain. The Russian horses, native-bred and of types seldom seen in the West, often perform extremely well despite no apparent international experience whatsoever except for the annual European, World, or Olympic competition.

Once every four years the Australians arrive on the Olympic scene with four horses. The Australian horses are among the best in the world; tough, fast, and athletic, they do surprisingly well. Until 1980, they had to be sold off after the Olympics because it was impossible to return them down under without a ruinously expensive six months' quarantine in England, the only country from which Australia would accept animals as being free from disease before the strict rules were relaxed.

But the Australians will be the first to admit that they don't train seriously. They will pick up a horse in the spring, run in a Novice event, try it in the Advanced levels, and if it goes well, they pack it up and send it off to the Olympics. Their horses are athletes, used and not babied. If the Australians ever get serious about training they will be a real threat.

Canada won the team medals in the World Championships in 1978 with four nice horses. The climate in Canada hampers the development of a regular circuit of events because the long northern winters linger until May, so the Canadians make the trek south to take advantage of the American events to prepare their teams. Since a series of coaches in the past few years has left the Canadian team without the central control over the sport enjoyed by their southern neighbors, it is still largely a bunch of individual riders who get together for the important competitions. Their win in Kentucky has been rewarded by new national interest in the sport.

America has found its answer in LeGoff. A definite style is stamped on his riders; an American style, similar to the style of the American jumping squad trained by de Nemethy. At the end of his first four years in America, LeGoff's plans bore fruit and the American team, programmed as never before, rode smoothly through the Burghley World Championships with the efficiency of an IBM computer, taking all the spoils of war with the team gold medals and also the individual gold and silver. "Like a Mercedes in a field of Minis," Lucinda Prior-Palmer said admiringly.

Just as Lafayette's regiments had swept the field at Yorktown in the final defeat of the British, LeGoff's riders shone like sunbursts at the World Championships. Another Frenchman had become an American hero.

4

The Eye of the Beholder

A head like a snake, a skin like a mouse,
An eye like a woman, bright, gentle and brown,
With loins and a back that would carry a house,
And quarters to lift him smack over a town

G. J. WHYTE-MELVILLE

I

There are perhaps some fifteen thousand horses in the world today that take part in three-phase competition, and nearly all of them compete only at the lower levels. Of these fifteen thousand, roughly a hundred can be classified as international horses, horses that are capable of jumping around an Olympic or a World Championships course; and of this elite hundred, maybe twenty-five can be classified as top horses. These are the horses with a chance of winning a gold medal, or even of placing in the top ten: one sixth of one per cent of all the possibles.

The search for a horse of such potential caliber leads down a complex of frustrating side roads. There are so many intangible elements concerned: not only must you find a prospect but, if its talents are to come to life, you must train it and must keep it in one piece while it (or you) develops the necessary skills through experience. If you are lucky enough to be possessed of an oil well you can go out and purchase a horse that is already competing at the top. This will cost anything over fifty thousand dollars — peanuts compared to what you would pay for a successful show jumper — but, even so, no amount of cash can shortcut the experience needed to ride the animal because experience can only be bought with time and hard work.

Given this time, and given that inflation has caught up with your checkbook, as it has with most of the world, you do what Bruce Davidson does: you buy a young horse and bring it along from the beginning. There are always around a dozen young horses at Chesterland Farm.

Bruce buys his young horses from a great friend and neighbor, Robert M. Tindle, a horseman who learned his craft as one of the remount buyers for the United States cavalry and who has developed it through prolonged experience in assessing young horses. Mr. Tindle, formerly the field master for Mr. Stewart's Cheshire Foxhounds, has for many

OPPOSITE: A relaxed moment at Chesterland Farm.

71

Each horse, whether it lives in, or out in the pasture, is checked over every day to accustom it to being handled.

years bought young horses for himself and for his friends and neighbors. He is a man who knows how to look at a gangling two-year-old and tell what it will look like as it matures. Bruce trusts him implicitly.

Being a world champion has its moments of reward, but it also has drawbacks. Wherever he goes, Bruce discovers people who want to sell him a horse which, they tell him, is "just perfect for everything." Nearly always these horses are vastly overrated and vastly overpriced, merely because people imagine that the champion of the world can afford nothing but the best.

For example, during a clinic he was giving on the West Coast, one of his students insisted that she had the ideal event horse. She told Bruce that the horse was 17 hands high, a fabulous mover and a fabulous jumper. At 8 P.M., having given lessons nonstop for twelve hours except for an hour off for lunch, Bruce went to look at this paragon. He remembers the horse well: "Here was this mammoth who looked like a prehistoric dinosaur. It might have been *papered* as a Quarter Horse, as my student had told me; but anything that was not Quarter Horse had to be Percheron. It moved quite well, but there was no way in which this huge beast could gallop around a three-day course. It might well have been called Thunder Thighs because of the way it went."

Mr. Tindle, Dr. Moyer (the Davidsons' veterinarian who takes a great interest in the young horses), Story Jenks, and Bruce watch intently as the young horses begin their jumping schooling.

For Bruce it was another blind alley — one he had been down too many times. Although he is always game to look at any horse he hears about, he really prefers to put his trust in one or two people, such as Mr. Tindle, whom he has learned to respect as judges and as horsemen.

An eye for a horse takes years to develop. The type of youngster that the World Champion likes is two or three years old, strong-bodied, but preferably on the thin side so that the basic bone structure shows clearly. Bruce looks for excellent feet, for a really good eye, and for movement and balance. He likes to see a young horse move at freedom in the field, as it will do much less under tack or with a tight girth around its middle. He looks for a strong, well-constructed hind leg, taking particular notice of where the hocks are placed. He feels that in the young horse, the overall impression is important; one must look at the undeveloped animal and get a feeling of what it will blossom into.

II

Chesterland Farm is an ideal training ground. The stables lie at the end of a long drive bordered by tall trees. On one side of the drive are two large permanent dressage arenas and a jumping area, and on the other side are rolling paddocks in which the youngsters spend their days grazing and playing. Jumping panels are set into the paddock fences.

The main stable is a long, low building with two rows of stalls. It has a large, well-organized tack room, a washing stall, and an overhead hayloft. Everything paintable is bright red and yellow, the Davidson colors. The flower tubs outside the doors are red and yellow, as are the

The two-year-olds watch over the fence as their three-year-old friends are led into the stable for work.

pitchforks, the brooms, the fat feed tubs, the saddle racks, the mounting block, and the small fire engine belonging to Buck, the Davidsons' first son, who was born in 1976. A second barn has been built next to the parking lot; and behind the two stables is a full-sized indoor riding hall and a turnout shed that houses the youngsters that are always on hand, eating and growing, waiting for their education.

The stables are busy from six in the morning to seven at night. In addition to their own string of six horses, Bruce and Carol have horses boarded by other people, several hunters, and one or two steeplechasers in training because both Bruce and Carol love to ride in the local point-to-points. The barn is kept immaculate by Bruce's head groom and an army of "gnomes" — working pupils who come with their own horses to be coached in return for work. Three small Jack Russell terriers dart in and out, and a flock of fighting cocks peck through the muck heaps. An added hazard is provided by Jethro, the peacock, who is given to displaying his tail, thereby pleasing his wife, Cleo, and horrifying horses new to the scene.

Bruce feels that constant handling of the young horses is deeply important. He begins with yearlings and two-year-olds living out in the fields, making sure that they are caught and handled every day so they

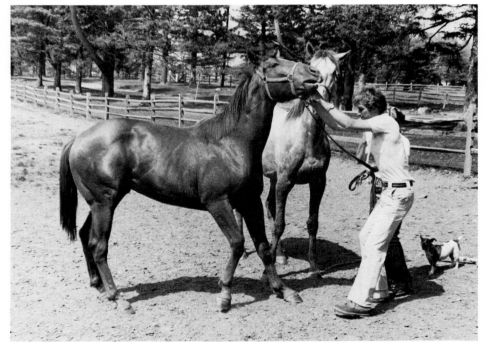

Bruce lunges his horses in a chambon, a schooling martingale that encourages them to lower their heads and use their back muscles correctly.

LEFT: The two-year-olds out in the pasture are treated regularly for parasites. Ailsa, the Jack Russell terrier, acts as overseer.

are accustomed to humans. This is the time to begin routine medical care, and the young horses' feet are conscientiously trimmed and shaped. Careful attention to these details in the early stages can prevent a great many future problems. The young horses are wormed on a regular schedule to keep them free from parasites, and any scrape or cut is treated at once.

The two-year-olds are lunged without fail for a half-hour to three-quarters of an hour a day in the indoor school and, later, in the outdoor ring until they are settled. They learn to walk and trot in a relaxed manner in groups or alone. After this they are hacked out in a group every day for three-quarters of an hour, riding in file head to tail with each one taking a turn to lead. They walk through water whenever possible and are made to step over small logs, learning to relax and get the humps out of their backs.

Basic training begins in May with the lunging. In July and August the youngsters are ridden out and hacked, and at the beginning of September they are turned out to pasture again until May of the following year, when they are brought back into work as three-year-olds and the whole process is repeated. Now more mature physically, they are lunged and hacked all summer, staying out in the field at night until the first of November, when they start to live in the stable routinely. After that date they live in, as opposed to living out at pasture, until the beginning of their four-year-old year, when their real training begins.

III

During his time at Gladstone, Bruce became fast friends with Harden Crawford and his wife, Ailsa, who lived in the big house next door to the main stable. Denny Crawford had his own very pronounced ideas about training horses, which he was applying to a young dark bay Thoroughbred mare in his stable — a horse in which he had purchased a half interest as a two-year-old as a subject for experiment.

The mare had been bought as a bet. One day Denny had been having a drink with his old friend Dr. Charles Reid, a veterinary surgeon, and had looked out of Reid's kitchen window to see a strapping two-year-old racing around the paddock.

"You know, Charley," he said thoughtfully, "you could take that youngster and make an Olympic or World Champion medal winner out of it."

"You must be out of your mind!" retorted Reid.

Denny asserted his belief that you could take any well-bred, well-made young Thoroughbred and be such a fanatic on teaching it the basic skills that it would be able to carry you around an Advanced three-day event. With, of course, a bit of luck. He bet that he could turn Charley Reid's homebred filly by Cormac out of Ballylicky into an Olympic horse. Reid, who thought his friend was crazy, took the bet.

Bruce sat and listened while Denny expounded his methods at the Gladstone dinner table. Denny held that if you painstakingly educated the horse so that it had complete confidence in the rider all through its training you could produce a completely reliable horse — not necessarily

OPPOSITE: Bruce and Tri-Corn show a close rapport.

76

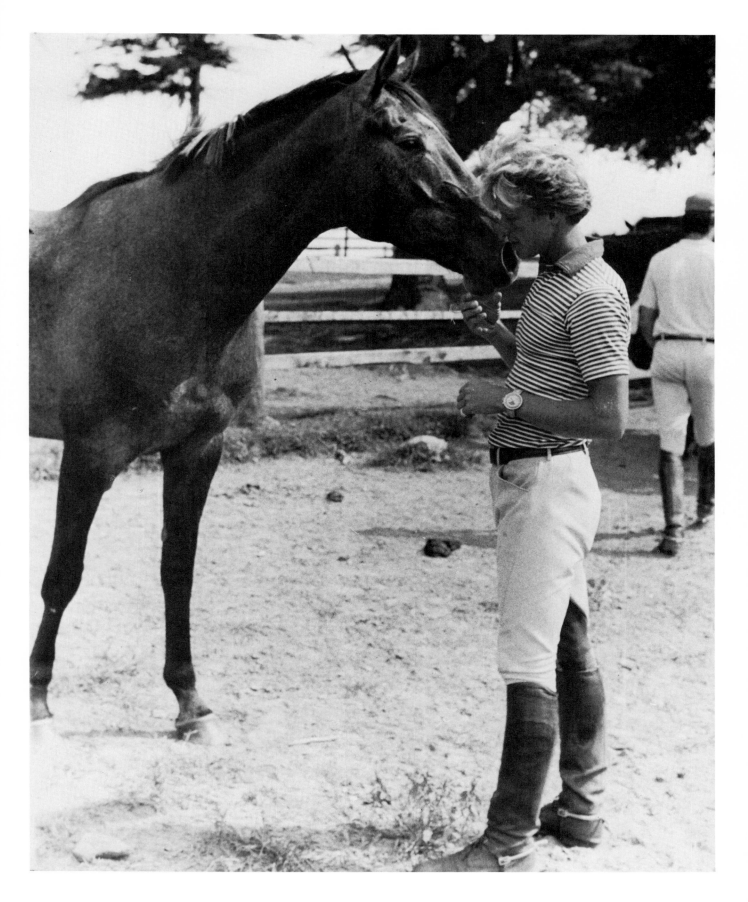

The young horses gallop out over the undulating Chesterland fields, head to tail.

a brilliant horse, but one that you could rely on entirely at any time. Bruce, who was new to the eventing world, thought that it was possible to teach a horse academically, but he wondered how you could have any faith that that horse would make no mistake on a championship course in view of the imponderables of weather and terrain. Yet the more he listened to Denny the more he realized that LeGoff, in *his* way, was saying the same thing.

Bruce rode the young horse when Denny went on holiday. She was Bally Cor. In 1976, ridden by Tad Coffin, she won the individual Olympic gold medal (and incidentally won Denny's bet).

Bruce never forgot his friend's ideas. He realized that a good cross-country horse is not the crazy horse that jumps because it is scared, or one that is too full of energy because it has been overfed, but the one that jumps because it understands the job at hand and can analyze and cope with the situation. This kind of horse jumps because by nature it is a very generous being, wanting to give the rider what is expected and trusting the rider not to ask more than it can do.

IV

In May of their four-year-old year, Bruce's youngsters begin more serious training. They are worked on the flat for an hour a day, learning to obey the aids, to be supple and relaxed in their bodies, and to come onto the bit. They are taught the suppling exercises that require them to move laterally away from the leg, and they learn to move with impulsion and rhythm, developing their muscles in regular, ordered workouts. Their balance under the rider improves and they begin to carry themselves with ease.

At the same time their work over fences starts, initially with trotting over cavalletti, which are spaced at set intervals to teach them control in jumping and to develop their back muscles. They are asked to jump some small fences — usually three-foot oxers — to see what their natural aptitude for jumping may be. Bruce watches carefully. If he has a group of young horses and one is having more problems than the others he studies it particularly to find out the cause of the problems. Is it age, awkwardness, or some conformation defect that has not been apparent before? If the horse shows no natural talent for jumping he will reject it as a three-day prospect; there is no point in forcing a horse to do work it has no aptitude for.

The four-year-olds receive a thorough grounding in flat work and are introduced to all types of cross-country obstacles. Each new type of fence, whether it be a drop, a ditch, a bank, a spread, or a vertical, is introduced in the training sessions, and the youngsters learn to deal with their feet and their own weight and that of their rider. In the beginning they jump straightforward, scaled-down versions of their ultimate goals, and as they become proficient they jump bigger, more complicated fences.

Bruce pays particular attention to introducing water fences. Streams and ponds are included on the daily hacks, and the string of young horses is routinely ridden down to the Brandywine River to spend hours paddling about to allay any fear of water. No horse is ever rushed, and care is taken to ensure that each understands one step before it moves onto the next. If a horse seems to be too phlegmatic about jumping, Bruce will send it out hunting in the autumn. "The object of this is to gas it up a little and teach it to be more aggressive," he says.

The horses begin their competition life in their five-year-old year. Once they have begun to compete, Bruce evaluates their potential as three-day horses, knowing that those that do well in the one-day trials are not necessarily going to make the grade as three-day horses. His continual search is for the really competitive horse — and the really competitive horse is almost never the easy one to deal with. The competitive horse is a prima donna who has to have things his own way a little: he has to be put in the van just so, and must have special consideration about whom he travels next to, or the way in which he is bandaged. It matters to him whether he goes into the van first or second and whether he comes off last or first, whether he gets a double stall or would rather be left alone, and whether he likes or loathes arriving early and being lunged to settle him down.

The competitive horse is therefore not the easiest one to deal with in terms of the hours you have to put into him, and he may not be the winner at the lower levels. Sometimes the rider must be willing to sacrifice a good dressage test in order to find out the more important facts

**David O'Connor on Arranshar
at the Penn-Del Fence, Chesterland 1979.**

1 2

4

4. The horse is concentrating on the second element.

5. The rider has allowed the reins to slip to help balance the animal and has compensated by taking up the slack in his arms to maintain the necessary contact.

6. The horse jumps safely out.

3

"The question posed by this fence is that it offers the option of taking a bounce downhill. It is absolutely essential in the approach to the fence that the horse meet it on an aggressive but bouncy stride. Galloping downhill tends to put a horse on its forehand."

1. The horse has met a good take-off point. The rider has his hands too low and braced on the withers.

2, 3. The horse appears to be a little too much on the forehand, and the rider is too far forward.

5   **6**

81

about the horse: can he gallop? is he clever? does he have the scope? Bruce looks for a horse that will carry him around a Preliminary course and still be pulling at the end, a horse that will take hold of the bit and say, "Right: come along with me!" He rejects the horse that says to him, "Gosh, this is hard work: leave me alone."

In the initial stages the horse's performance in the dressage phase is relatively unimportant, since the main requirement for a three-day horse is that he be able to run and jump. By the time he enters his first three-day event the horse must show that he is unimpressed with the size of the Preliminary fences and that he can jump them at speed.

Bruce prefers to find out early on whether the horse has what it takes to make it into the big time because there are only so many hours in each day and only so many days in each week, and he wants to spend those hours and days with horses that have real potential. The essential ingredients for a three-day horse are boldness, movement, speed, and scope; if a horse shows that he is lacking any one of these ingredients, no amount of time can make up the lack. There is no bluffing in the search for a really good horse, and those that do not measure up are not worth spending time with. Bruce is ruthlessly honest about each horse, but if he believes that a horse has all the ingredients, even if it is difficult in the early stages of training, he will invest any amount of time waiting for the horse to settle and realize its true potential. "If it is there, someday it will come out," he says.

The true international three-day horse must show a great deal of raw talent. It may be high-strung and nervous but must not be neurotic — there is a difference. Each horse is not necessarily going to be an all-rounder. Some show more adaptability for one discipline than the others; some are better dressage horses, others are better hunters or show jumpers or even steeplechasers. The three-day horse must show the potential for doing all the phases brilliantly.

By no means are the jumps on the cross-country courses natural to a horse; no horse would go out of its way to jump them by itself. Yet, once the horse is trained, it should be able to handle fences with ease. How many people can perform the intricate movements of the ballet dancer? Those who can, and who have the will, do not mind pushing their bodies hard until they can do those movements, and in the same way the athletic horse can be taught to use its body to the fullest capacity.

A rider who asks things that are not fair to a particular horse, so that it falls or stops because it is trying to make efforts that are beyond its natural ability, should question what he is doing. There is no point in putting all the time and effort and pain into training a horse that is going to let you down because it doesn't have the talent required of an international three-day horse.

People have the image of Bruce Davidson as the World Champion, and each time he appears in competition he is expected to win. Yet although it is difficult to demonstrate a champion image on a young, untried horse, Bruce is willing to sacrifice his image because he is dealing with his own time and money. He cannot spare two years to find out about each horse, even though this wait would let him be sure of winning. As it is, he may have an occasional stop or fall, but it helps him to find out if the horse's instincts are right. Does the horse have a sense of self-preservation? Does it have the intelligence to pay attention when the pressure is on?

V

During the miserable months of 1975 when Irish Cap stood in his stall fighting for breath, Bruce looked constantly for horses. The youngsters were coming along nicely, but none, as yet, showed the charisma of his faithful champion. As the weeks and months went by, Irish Cap began to recover, helped by the familiar surroundings and his tenacious will to win life back. Slowly, he defeated the lung infection and began to breathe more easily. On a bright day late in the fall, when the leaves had turned to amber and the air was cool and crisp, he was able to leave his confinement; but it had taken a whole year, and Bruce knew that even if his horse could make it to the Olympic Games the following September he might not be able to hold out long enough to defend his title at the next World Championships, which were then three years ahead. He hoped with fervent love that these pessimistic thoughts of his were wrong, but underneath he knew that perhaps he was dreaming the impossible.

One day Mr. Tindle called, telling Bruce that he had been on a horse-buying trip in the Western states and had picked up a nice big young horse that he thought Bruce would like. Bruce politely thanked him and said that he would get over to look at the new prospect as soon as he had time. But it was a busy year: he had the ride on Golden Griffin, one of the USET horses, at the Ledyard Farm international event, and after that he went on to the Pan American Games.

When eventually he returned to Chesterland, Mr. Tindle called again. "This horse is too much for the people who bought him," he said. "I may be making a mistake, but I think this is a really high-quality horse with a lot of potential."

It was late in October 1975 when Bruce at last found enough time to look at the horse. Jack LeGoff was also in the neighborhood, staying with Bruce and Carol for the last big event of the season, the Radnor Hunt three-day competition. "I've got a horse to look at," Bruce told him. "Perhaps you would like to come with me. It is stabled just down the road from here."

LeGoff is never reluctant to look at potentially good team horses, so the two arranged to meet the moment the Radnor day was over. They drove up to the house after dark. A big, angular gray horse with a lot of bone and an enormous head was trotted out for their inspection in front of the headlights of the truck. The little they could see impressed them, and they agreed to return next day to look some more.

On the following morning Bruce and LeGoff returned to examine the horse in daylight. They watched as the young daughter rode him around the field. Bruce mounted the big gray to test the feel for himself. It was not long before he rode over to LeGoff.

"Jack, this is a terrific horse. It's not even trying. It knows nothing — and look at it!"

"I know, my friend. He is all the things I would want for a horse of

**Bruce Davidson on Ten Eighty
at King Brian's Walk, Chesterland 1979.**

1 2

4

4. Here he is well over, having made perhaps too much effort in jumping too high. This gives a slightly awkward effect as his knees are already unfolding, but he is well clear of the fence.

5. The horse undergoes tremendous concussion on landing, and the hindquarters are well under the body.

6. The first stride of gallop away is very strong with the horse back in balance and going on towards the final fence.

3

"This jump is a footbridge set over a small stream. The ground descends into it giving a slightly deceptive ground line because of the water underneath, but the fence is basically a parallel oxer. This is a time for the rider to consider jumping over a point to help the horse stand off, and to avoid getting in too close and hitting the front rail with the knees, much like the Serpent in Kentucky. This is a fence that needs to be ridden with a very forward and positive attitude."

1. Ten Eighty is alert and analyzing the situation.

2. A good point of take-off.

3. The horse is well up into the air, making an exceptional effort over a reasonably demanding next-to-last fence on course.

5   **6**

mine." LeGoff purchased the horse and he was shipped up to the team headquarters. Six weeks later LeGoff sold the horse to Bruce because team policy dictated that the coach should not own a horse.

The big gray arrived at Chesterland. The working students craned their necks for a glimpse of the latest acquisition. They were dismayed. Off the van walked this enormous horse with an oversized head, long gangling legs, an upside-down neck, and a fiery eye.

"What has Bruce bought himself this time?" they wondered. "He looks just like a duck. Old Duckface," they said mockingly. The official registration papers called him Might Tango, but the horse became "Ducky" to everyone at Chesterland.

Irish Cap, the complete gentleman and diplomat, watched the stranger walk into the aisle and took an instant dislike to him. Might Tango didn't care. Soon it became obvious that he didn't care about anyone. He was brash, intense, and opinionated, and he had so much energy that he could not handle it. He swung around in his stall, looking for something to keep him occupied. He threw his buckets into the aisle and refused to eat his hay, insisting that it be left out in front of his stall so that he could observe everything that was going on. He attacked any horse he was turned out with. Bruce settled down to study this *enfant terrible* and to find a way into his mind.

The first time he tried to lunge the horse, Tango turned in on him and ran towards him, standing on his hind feet and striking out at Bruce's head, thinking it was time to play.

"No one else is to lunge this horse," Bruce told his students firmly. "He's too unsettled, and much too strong."

He got on and tried to ride the horse, looking for a way to communicate with it. Tango had been raced on the small half-mile tracks out West at a very early age, and all he knew was racing. As is often the case with horses after a racing career, the young horse was tightly cranked. It took the best part of two years to settle him down. Yet the horse had so much sheer ability that Bruce knew that if it could be controlled Tango would become a fantastic horse.

The first year with Might Tango would have deterred a lesser rider. Bruce knew that this was an exceptional horse, and sometimes he would have a flash of the potential quality. "He gave me fleeting moments of greatness," he says. "They totaled perhaps two minutes in the whole first year."

He decided that it might be a good idea to see how the horse would react to an actual competition, and so he made an entry for a Novice horse trials. It started disastrously: Might Tango, thinking he was going back to the racetrack, almost destroyed the van in transit and, on arrival, fell off the ramp in a fit of temperament. It took everyone's efforts to get a saddle onto him. Bucking, rearing, more on two legs than on four, he said very clearly, "Let's get on with it. Where's the starting gate?"

Just as Bruce was resigned to taking him home he settled down and produced a reasonable dressage test, went clean over the cross-country fences (the first he had ever seen, as Bruce had been unable to get him out beforehand), and also went clean in the stadium. He won the event.

Successive competitions were equally traumatic, since Might Tango

OPPOSITE: Might Tango and Jane Cobb have established a deep affection. The big intense horse is totally relaxed with the young Yorkshire girl.

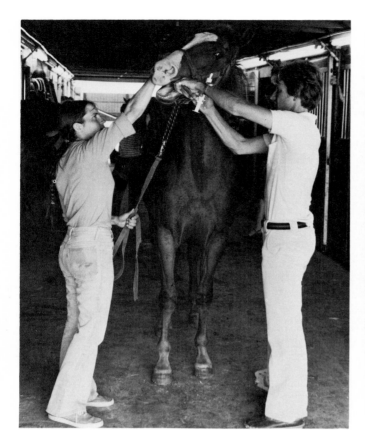

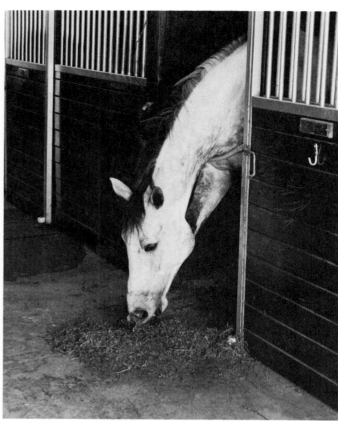

This horse is being wormed with a paste gun.

RIGHT: Might Tango insists on eating his hay from the aisle in front of his stall so that he can keep an eye on everything that happens.

was highly unsettled when away from home. Bruce worked for hours in public trying to settle him for dressage while experienced observers on the circuit shook their heads, convinced that this time the champion had made a bad mistake. "The horse is crazy," they said. "He'll never settle."

VI

In training all of his horses, Bruce had always tried to do everything as he had been taught, believing deeply that the classical way, though time-consuming, was the only way. He had never resorted to gadgets to help him to put his young horses into a correct frame; but he realized that there would always be an exception to every rule he had learned and that the rider must cope with each individual problem as it arises. Some horses, for example, had been ruined in their early training, while others had unusual dispositions.

"You cannot say, 'I will never do this; or never do that,'" Bruce says. "*Never* is a long time. When you have to get a result from a horse you do it the best way you can.

"All horses have to be presented, ultimately, in the same way. They have to come from behind onto your hand and work. There are more ways than one to put a horse between your hands and legs and onto the bit. Ultimately you have to produce the correct result."

Might Tango was a horse to flout all rules. He needed exceptional

training. He was so powerful that Bruce could not hold him in training gallops, so he trained him in a Western hackamore — a tight noseband that acts on a horse's nose instead of on his mouth — and strapped his head down with a standing martingale: unconventional in the extreme, but it worked. Now that Tango is further along in his training Bruce is able to use a simple egg-butt snaffle bit instead.

Initially, the horse disdained the lower-level cross-country fences, flipping over them without attention: they were, it seemed, beneath his notice. Wondering how to teach his horse to look at his fences, Bruce took the deliberate risk of putting Might Tango in too close to a three-foot tire jump in the hope that he would take a fall. The horse hit the fence hard, twisting so badly that Bruce came flying off — yet Tango put down a fifth leg and saved himself, showing the first sign of his uncanny ability to get himself out of trouble.

Bruce on Might Tango leading the youngsters out for their galloping session at Chesterland Farm.

"All horses eventually have to come onto the bit from behind." Bruce on one of his latest prospects, J. J. Babu, at Chesterland 1979.

OPPOSITE: A mass of equipment must accompany the event rider to competition. Jane holds Irish Cap and Might Tango, the two champions, at the barn at Chesterland with their tack and stable gear spread out in front of her.

So Bruce worked on, trying to find the key to this temperamental artist. And then, at the end of 1977, Might Tango found a friend. Jane Cobb, a young English girl, arrived at Chesterland to take over the duties of head groom, and she and Might Tango fell instantly in love. The big, restless horse had at last found someone who appreciated his insatiable curiosity and who would think up games for him to play and talk to him and baby him. He began to settle, to stop his ceaseless stall-walking, and to eat his food. The more mischief he could find, the more Jane laughed at him and loved him.

The training routines at Chesterland follow the seasons. Winter is a time for rest and for reinforcement of learned disciplines, spring is a time for fitting up and competition, and summer is a holiday before the autumn circuit begins. After strenuous competitions the horses have a break to renew their energy — all horses, that is, except Might Tango. Might Tango, with his restless energy, his overwhelming strength and talent, and all his idiosyncrasies, went into training at the beginning of 1976 and stayed in training for two and a half years nonstop.

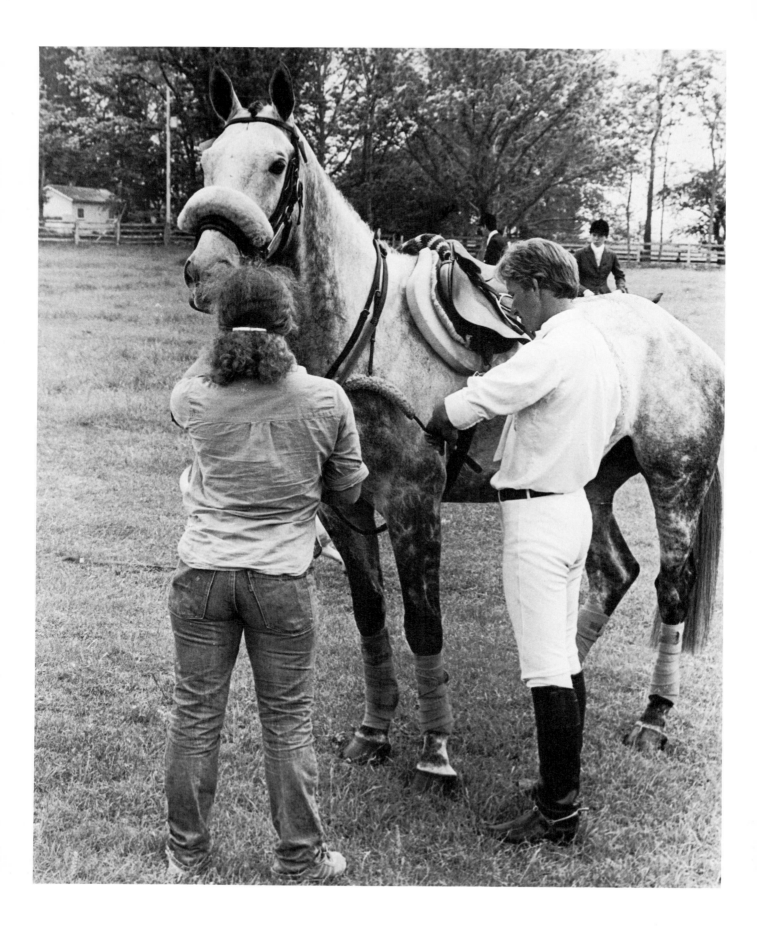

5

Interval Training

Long quiet rides settle a spirited horse down, but do
not expect him to quieten by riding fast and far. Do
not let him gallop at full speed.

XENOPHON, *Manual of Equitation*

I

Long-distance runners have been using interval training to condition
themselves for many years, but it took Jack LeGoff, who had ridden both
racehorses and endurance horses, to adapt this scientific conditioning
program to three-day event horses. Interval training is based on a few
simple principles which riders need to know, and a great deal of complicated physiology which, happily, horsemen can manage perfectly well
without knowing in minute detail.

Any sustained physical effort uses energy, which is released through
the muscles. As energy is used up, lactic acid builds up in the system.
This acid needs to be removed and recycled by oxygen in the blood
otherwise the muscles lose their elasticity and begin to ache. When a
surfeit of lactic acid is present, the muscles tire so much that they are
prone to injury. In the fit horse the heart and lungs work at top capacity,
pumping the blood carrying the oxygen through the system to the muscles; this oxygen converts the lactic acid back into energy in the form of
glycogen. Horses are vulnerable to serious injuries when there is an
insufficient circulation of oxygen to their muscles, causing the muscles
to tire and the stress to be taken by the ligaments.

Luckily you do not need a degree in biochemistry to monitor your
horse's fitness because three vital signs will do this for you: the horse's
temperature and his pulse and respiration rates. As the horse works, the
activity of the heart and lungs is stepped up to replace the energy that is
being used. The object of interval training is to increase the capacity of
the heart and lungs by building their strength slowly and systematically,
so that they can replace used energy in the shortest amount of time
possible and can return to normal rates. Interval training alternates periods
of stress with periods of rest when the heart and lungs are allowed
partially to recover before being restressed, thereby gradually enlarging
these organs' capacity for recovery. Old-fashioned methods used periods

OPPOSITE: A vital part of interval training is knowing how to check the
horse's pulse and respiration rates and
to gauge the fitness. Bruce checks
Might Tango's heart rate at Blue
Ridge.

93

The long galloping stride of the event horse. J. J. Babu at Chesterland 1979.

of exertion with no rest and repetition to build resistance, which was dangerous because the system could accidentally be overstressed. In interval training the rider can be sure of an accurate check on the horse's state of recovery merely by counting the pulse and respiration numbers.

To establish a program of interval training the rider must first check on the normal temperature (T), pulse (P), and respiration (R) of the horse at rest. Most horses will have a normal T ranging between 100° and 101° Fahrenheit, a normal R of 10 to 15 breaths a minute, and a normal P of 35 to 40 beats a minute. The T is taken with a rectal thermometer. The R can be counted by watching the horse's flank move in and out (each in-and-out movement counts for one breath), or by placing the hand lightly over one nostril and counting the exhalations. The pulse can be found by touch between the branches of the jawbones, or, alternatively, with a stethoscope over the heart on the horse's left side, just behind the

A great deal of time is spent at a desk planning the daily work schedule and the competition season.

elbow. Take a count for fifteen seconds if, as often happens, the horse is fidgety, and multiply by four to find the rate per minute.

The basic principle of interval training is to work the horse, check the increase in the P and R rates, rest the horse for a short interval so that the heart and lungs partially recover, then stress the horse by working again. The reason for the check on the P and R is to see how quickly the horse returns to normal. Should the horse take an unreasonable length of time to return to normal, taking into consideration the length of the work, the speed, and the type of terrain, and of course the weather, it is being overstressed, and work must be reduced until the rates recover. The objective, simply but beautifully, is to increase resistance to fatigue by increasing the efficiency of the circulatory system through scientific conditioning.

Interval training can only succeed if the rider knows how far and how

The long and the short of it. Bruce and Might Tango tower above Mary Anne Tauskey and Marcus Aurelius, the "bionic pony," proof that eventers and their horses come in all shapes and sizes.

Cooling out the horse on a hot day takes a great deal of water and a great many willing hands.

fast the horse is working. The number of intervals between gallops and the speed and distance of each workout must be carefully controlled so that the rider can build the horse up to optimum effort over the distance required for any competition. The weather, of course, will affect the numbers. Some horses labor in the heat and are dynamite in the crisp and cold. You have to know if your horse can handle heat and must adjust your program accordingly. The challenge of conditioning is that all these factors must be considered.

Interval training principles are used throughout the conditioning work, and the galloping work is generally done every fourth day. The reason for this is that a horse's system takes four days after a gallop to take the full benefit and recover from the exertion, so it is at precisely this point that another workout is needed to build up on the earlier one. If the horse was galloped again after only two or three days there would be the risk of overstressing it because its body would not have had enough time to recover. Conversely, if the gallop was left to the fifth day, the horse would have more time than is advantageous to the conditioning program. The galloping part of interval training is therefore a gradual process of buildup.

Ideally, an interval training program can be carefully prepared for each individual horse; but in actuality one has to be ready to deal with the unexpected — the horse may lose a shoe one day and the rider may be unable to get hold of the farrier for three days, so a gallop is missed; or the horse gets a slight injury and has to be laid off hard work for a week, or it develops a cold or cough and cannot gallop for two weeks. The customary training program for an international three-day horse is based on a fifteen-week plan, but it is just as well to allow a couple of extra weeks to deal with the mishaps that nearly always occur.

Depending upon the individual needs of each horse, the day after galloping is usually an "easy" day. The horse will walk out, perhaps with a short trot now and again, to unstiffen its tired muscles. The next two days will be spent in more strenuous exercise, practicing dressage or jumping and going for long, steady hacks up and down hills. Conditioning includes a great deal of foundation work, upon which the interval training merely serves as the top story.

Before interval training at the gallop can begin the horse must have been in work for at least six weeks, including walking out in the country, working on the flat for up to an hour a day, and conditioning at the trot up hills. It needs to have some base muscle before the interval gallops begin.

II

The countryside surrounding Chesterland is ideal for conditioning horses. There are miles of long, gradual hills — rolling countryside that builds muscles and lungs. Bruce believes that nothing can ever replace these long, slow works in giving body and depth to a horse's condition. If the horse is trained on a flat track or without hills, more fast works have to be included to put it on its toes. Even so, it does not have the same depth to its conditioning because nothing, unfortunately, can beat rolling country for true fitness.

"The work effect created by working up hills affects not only the muscles, making the hindquarters strong, but it also develops the lungs," Bruce explains. "A gradual uphill work develops the lungs without an increase of speed and has the same effect as fast work. If you have a very hilly area with long, slow pulls uphill, you do not need much speed to produce a proper lung function. If you have a flatter area you must use quicker, sharper works to keep the horse's wind up to the strength needed to compete, even in one-day events. Some people train on sand tracks or even turf tracks on the flat, but it is just not the same as galloping up a hill."

Both Irish Cap and Might Tango were trained for the World Championships using interval training methods, though their programs were varied according to their personalities. In training Irish Cap in 1974, first for Badminton in the spring and then for Burghley in the fall, Bruce faithfully applied the system he had learned from LeGoff. Since Irish Cap is a big-bodied horse who will work hard no matter what speed he goes, Bruce set up a program of long, slow canters at a speed of 400 meters per minute (about 15 miles per hour). Irish Cap could gallop at quite a good speed over quite a good distance, and the steeplechase speed required in three-day competition — 690 meters per minute (about 26 miles an hour) — was within his range; but Bruce knew that this speed was his top limit and that there could be no "stepping on the gas" to pick up an additional ten seconds or so. Therefore Irish Cap would need a solid foundation of slow, muscle-building works.

"Badminton, basically, is an individual cross-country race," Bruce says. "You can't hope to win there if you can't make the time. I had Irish Cap built up as strong as possible before I gave him any wind works to be sure that he would be able to carry himself and not become muscle-tired. I feel sure that when a horse becomes muscle-tired it starts to run on its ligaments and increases the risks of breaking down."

Irish Cap was built up over a period of fifteen weeks, cantering at 400 mpm for three minutes with a three-minute break, followed by another three-minute canter, a three-minute break, finishing with a third three-minute interval canter. Within two months the length of the canters had slowly increased until he was doing three ten-minute canters, still at 400 mpm; and this was *before* he began doing any faster gallops.

Once Cap could cope with the three ten-minute intervals easily, he had two sharper works in the month before the competition, one four weeks ahead of the cross-country and one three weeks ahead. He did six minutes at 400 mpm; a three-minute break; five minutes at 400 mpm, building up to 550 mpm for one minute; another three-minute break; then three minutes at 400 mpm, one minute at 550 mpm, one minute at 400 mpm, and one minute at 690 mpm consecutively. This made a work program based on six-minute intervals, but with varying speeds. Eight days and four days before each competition Irish Cap had a half mile pipe-opener uphill, galloping as fast as he could, with another pipe-opener after the dressage in a three-day competition.

Because of his horse's lung condition, Bruce took exceptional care to ensure that Irish Cap's living quarters were kept free from dust. Since the horse was a greedy eater, he had a strict diet to keep his weight down, getting approximately twelve quarts of grain and very little hay. His schedule was carefully planned and he followed a strict routine, going out early each morning since he was very sensitive to temperature and Bruce did not like to work him in extremes of hot or cold air.

On the other hand, Might Tango's schedule leading up to the 1978 World Championships was anything but routine. Whereas Irish Cap went to England as an Advanced level horse and was prepared for Badminton and Burghley in the conventional sequence, Might Tango started 1978 as a Preliminary level horse with an unorthodox background. He earned enough points to step up into the Advanced divisions so quickly that he was forced to run at that level at Ledyard in June and had then only two weeks before Chesterland's Advanced division. "You don't get much of a chance to do the proper gallops in two weeks," Bruce remarked.

Often under the pressures of training, horses require the additional assistance of whirlpool treatment. This is the barn at Chesterland Farm, with Might Tango watching on the right.

The young horses prepare for their gallops watched by Bruce and Might Tango.

However, Might Tango had a tremendous base of muscle-building works behind him. He had worked for two years without a holiday and he had spent hours of trotting up and down hills to settle him down, since he was so difficult to gallop. Might Tango was on a basic interval program, albeit a very flexible one; Bruce admits that he planned his programs instinctively for the intense, excitable young horse. "If a day came along and it seemed as if he would benefit from galloping I would gallop that day, because who knew what the next day would bring!" The horse had been worked all winter in the indoor school in a chambon, a schooling martingale that brings the horse's head down to a point where the back muscles are properly exercised. He was worked up to doing three six-minute intervals at a slow canter, which by Might

Tango's standards is about 500 mpm. He is a horse with great natural speed, needing little in the way of faster workouts. Fast work excites and upsets him, so he gets only one fast work before a major competition and a very brief pipe-opener after his dressage test.

In contrast to Irish Cap's strict diet, Might Tango is programmed to put on weight; his intensity burns off every spare ounce. He receives as much as twenty quarts of grain a day and in addition is led out to graze and is given as much hay as he will eat. Shortly before going to Kentucky, Bruce was very concerned about the young horse because each time he was worked hard he would come back in with a very high temperature. "He gave us quite a fright. We eventually discovered that because we had been leaving him out all night to eat the rich grass it was affecting his metabolism. We curtailed the turnouts and it made a definite difference."

Might Tango has a more efficient heart-lung system than Irish Cap. The most Might Tango had to gallop to reach the same fitness as his stablemate was three eight-minute gallops as opposed to Irish Cap's ten-minute works.

Interval training is of immense value to riders, but it needs to be custom tailored to each horse. Using the built-in checking system, any rider can come up with a program of work for any horse. Interval training may have a scientific base, but it takes an artist to apply it with ultimate effectiveness.

6

Course and Effect

A good cross-country course is a carefully planned series of obstacles not exceeding the prescribed dimensions, built on a track of the prescribed length over varied terrain. A bad cross-country course is a carefully planned series of obstacles not exceeding the prescribed dimensions, built on a track of the prescribed length over varied terrain.

ROGER HALLER, designer of the
1978 World Championships course

I

A peculiarity of eventing is that competitors train for months and years without having a precise knowledge of what they are training for until they arrive at the actual competition and inspect the cross-country course.

The challenge of each competition is controlled solely by the imagination of the course designer, whose job is to lay out a course that challenges both the scope of a horse and the skills of its rider. A good designer takes the efforts he is asking and spaces them around the course, placing the demanding complexes carefully, using the extra efforts of the uphill and downhill stretches with a calculated balance, deciding where the horse can be asked to gallop and when its rider must be cautious. He must offer alternatives to test the rider's judgment of his horse's ability to jump the obstacles in the fastest, shortest way possible (the fastest way is usually not the easiest way). The rider must then decide in advance how much he can expect of the horse on course as these problems are presented and must have alternative approaches up his sleeve, depending upon how his horse is coping with each test as it negotiates the course. The designer has to come up with a complete test of horse and rider, so that the best ones rise to the top like cream.

"No magic answer exists," wrote Roger Haller. "Mistakes can be made any place in the designing, planning, and construction and preparation of a course. If such mistakes are made you will end up with a bad cross-country course . . .

"There are four absolutely essential elements to consider. First the actual galloping track must utilize and fit into the terrain, depending upon

OPPOSITE: Bruce leads Irish Cap to the veterinary inspection at Montreal during the Olympic Games in 1976.

**Bruce Davidson on Wasyl
at Segal's Crossing, Chesterland 1979.**

1, 2. The horse has come to a good point of take-off for the ditch in the first part of the combination of ditch–vertical rail–ditch. The vertical rail was only ten feet beyond the ditch.

3. The horse's head is too high, interrupting the line between the bit, the rider's hands, and the top of his hip.

4. As the horse rises to the vertical rails, observe the placement of the hind legs and the power required to make this effort.

5. Over the top of the rails the horse catches sight of the far ditch and is alert to the third part of the combination. Rider is close and secure, ready to assist.

6, 7. Good continuity with the horse and rider well in balance, the rider encouraging him towards the last element.

8. At the point of take-off everything is very much in order.

9. Well over the ditch, and the attention of both horse and rider is on where they are going next.

2 3

6 7

9

105

what the site offers. Second, obstacles must be selected that will test the skills of horse and rider at the particular level of experience for the competition. Third, the site of the obstacles must not negate the intended purpose of the test — for example, a big spread galloping fence should not be sited coming off a sharp turn, or in a grove of trees with a poor approach. Fourth, the obstacles must be constructed of heavy, solid, and varied materials."

In certain parts of the world there is a fifth element: the climate. Serious mistakes have been made when the weather has not been properly considered. For example, in Mexico the course for the Olympic Games in 1968 was built on a golf course that offered ideal footing — except that, unfortunately, torrential rains fell every afternoon. Some of the riders might well have thought themselves candidates for their country's swimming teams as they struggled through swollen streams that swept the horses off their feet.

Bruce has seen most of the major international courses of the 1970s. He has a panoramic view of the trends in course design, not only in the United States, where eventing was a stepchild until the American victory in 1974, but also in Europe, where eventing has been widely established since the Second World War.

His international career started in 1972, at the Munich Olympic Games, on a course that introduced a plan for using multiple complexes of fences that has been imitated and expanded ever since.

Munich 1972

Munich was perhaps an ideal Olympic course because those riders who had less experienced or slower horses were offered a fair option at most fences, while those who were expert enough to take a risk could prove their quality. There was nearly always a more cautious route through the real problems, whereas the fast and bold horses could make a bit of time if they were presented accurately. This is a very important consideration in an Olympic trial, since allowance must be made for competitors who come from countries where eventing barely exists and who have therefore had very little chance to practice.

The focus was on elaborate bank combinations; the course required control and obedience, which suited the German style of horse and was not so natural to the big, galloping Thoroughbred of the British and American teams. The bogey complex of the course, which was confusing for many horses, was a bank-and-rail complex set in the woods with difficult distances between the obstacles and variations of jumping into light, into darkness, and into light again.

Yet it was not a course that demanded the impossible. It was consistent, it was well conceived and well built, and it tested the riders as much as, if not more than, the horses.

Badminton

"The art of designing a good course is to frighten the wits out of the riders on their feet, but not to hurt the horses on the day," claims Frank Weldon, Badminton's mastermind, whose course designs put pressure on riders. British riders were supreme for years because they had regular practice in analyzing such big, complicated courses. Badminton takes a good horse to get around, and furthermore it needs a thinking rider.

**Michael Tucker on Ben Wyvis
at Badminton.**

1. The stride before the take-off both horse and rider are in balance. They appear to be quite ready and concentrating.

2. Good jump. The rider fixes his hands a little on the horse's neck.

3. Over the top of the fence the horse is slightly flat in his back; the rider is slightly behind but secure and encouraging.

1

2

3

4

4. The landing is very much in balance, with the rider supporting the horse.

Continued overleaf.

5. Michael Tucker encourages Ben Wyvis for the take-off onto the bank.

6. The horse has met a good take-off point. This picture illustrates the tremendous strength, effort, and power required in jumping up — notice the hocks.

7

7, 8. Onto the bank. The horse is having a quick look at the far side which he was unable to see on the take-off. The rider is tight and secure and ready to assist.

9. As the horse prepares to jump down, the rider looks ahead to be able to drive the horse in the most direct line.

10. The shock of landing causes a slight loss of balance in the rider who falls too far forward, and he gets a negative reaction from the horse, who has a sour look on his face.

11. Concussion of landing. The rider is giving the necessary support for a horse coming off a drop fence.

10   **11**

6

8   9

Traditionally, it is bigger than an Olympic course. It has the stature of a World Championships.

The World Championships course was ideal. It had combinations of accuracy questions and boldness questions at complexes such as the Dairy Rails, which required a controlled jump up a steep slope, a left-handed turn, and a big jump out over a drop from uneven ground. It had gymnastic questions at the tight Sunken Road, and jumping and boldness questions at the Trout Hatchery, which was approached from a downhill slope. It had the Double Coffin for cleverness and surprise fences like the Waterloo Rails, which were approached over a group of moguls and which presented a big rail in front of very unlevel ground. The course required horses that were willing, "scopy," fast, and bold.

The terrain was more demanding than at Badminton, which is flat. Burghley had long, gentle downhill gallops and long pulls uphill, without

Burghley 1974

109

Neil Ayer, president of the United States Combined Training Association and the man behind the big international three-day event at Ledyard Farm in Massachusetts.

sharp climbs that there had been in Munich, or the treacherous footing that was later to be met at Montreal. While the green English turf begged for the imprint of hooves, not one single fence out of the thirty-two was a giveaway or a fill-in, and not once could the rider sit back and say, "This is nothing." From beginning to end the course demanded respect.

Ledyard Ledyard has developed over the years from a Pony Club National Rally course in the late 1960s into America's premier international course. It is located on the grounds of one of America's great houses, in Massachusetts just north of Boston, and it has earned its place among the truly international courses of the world because the owner, Neil Ayer, has designed a testing, technical course of immense scope.

Since the terrain at Ledyard is seldom level, it is more tiring than the big open courses. The roads and tracks are terribly rocky and muddy and are perhaps the worst on the international circuit, although Phase A at Badminton can be rough.

Climate can play havoc with its footing. In summer, Ledyard can become a cauldron of heat and humidity, while in autumn it can fall prey to the infamous "nor'easters" that blow in from the cold Atlantic and dump inches of rain overnight.

In 1975, Ledyard went fully international for the first time. Princess Anne, Mark Phillips, and a dozen other European riders who were great names in the eventing world flew their horses across the Atlantic to see how the Americans did on their home ground.

110

The American press, eager to pick up a royal story, followed the Princess all over like a pack of beagles who have viewed a hare. The Secret Service men who had been assigned to guard her were not prepared for the fitness of an event rider, and as Princess Anne went out for the fourth time to inspect the cross-country course her escort radioed urgently for a replacement. In trying to keep up with her he had blistered both feet severely.

Story Jenks on Toughkenamon over the double-brush oxer at Ledyard 1978.

Montreal 1976

The course designed for the Olympic Games was a great disappointment. The terrain was hilly and uneven, and the footing was varied all the way round. The course itself was best described as trappy; it needed clever horses but not "scopy" horses, and it did little to reward a horse who jumped big and bold. Riders found it difficult to develop any flow and rhythm on course because the fences forced them to turn and pull, turn and stop. There was nowhere for the horses to settle so that they could take the fences in stride.

Late in the course there were three big steps leading onto a small hill with a steep slope down behind it and a small log pile at the bottom that had little approach room. The horses struggled up the steps, gasped for breath, and fell down the steep slope, piling into the logs. It was a poorly conceived obstacle to be placed toward the end of a tremendously tiring test.

Unlike Munich, Montreal lacked consistency and fluency. It was a step back in course design.

111

3 **2**

7 **6**

Bruce Davidson on Irish Cap at the Montreal Olympics 1976.

1

1. Irish Cap is in open gallop, well balanced one stride away from the fence, his hocks coming well underneath him.

2. Irish Cap meets the fence on a long take-off stride. I am keeping him between my hand and leg.

3. He rises to the jump in good balance with his hocks right under him.

4, 5. Airborne. A good example of Irish Cap's scope, which is why I was not concerned about meeting this wide fence a bit long.

6. Note the impact of landing and the ease with which Irish Cap cleared the widest fence on the course.

7. The stride after landing his weight is thrust forward due to the speed and effort required, and I am in the required position for supporting his head to assist him.

5   **4**

The dreary weather cannot dampen the enthusiasm of the Queen and other members of the royal family as they watch Princess Anne in action at the Olympic Games in Montreal.

BELOW: A serious moment in any international event, the Ground Jury and the veterinarians examine the horses on the morning of the stadium jumping day. Tad Coffin holds Bally Cor for inspection at the Montreal Olympic Games.

One of the responsibilities of being a champion.

Mary Anne Tauskey (USA) riding The Sheik through the water in Kentucky 1979.

1. As the horse sees the water he has a very strong idea of stopping. It looks as if he has planted all four feet, which indicates he is considering not going at all.

2. As he jumps into the water from a standstill he has to make a greater effort than normal.

3. The descent to the water is extremely steep because he lacked forward motion. His back legs are on the top rail.

4. As his front feet land, the rider falls forward, and her right leg comes up on the saddle.

5. The horse veers to the right, leaving the rider entirely on the left side of the saddle.

6, 7, 8. The ultimate result: splash.

116

2

4 **5**

7 **8**

Lady Hugh Russell, who is paralyzed after a hunting accident, never misses the opportunity to inspect every inch of the international courses in her specially converted "mini-moke." She can get around as well as most people and a great deal faster. Here she inspects the water complex at Lexington.

II

Roger Haller, a young New Jersey businessman, was given the assignment of designing the World Championships course in Lexington's Kentucky Horse Park. Haller had been brought up in the foxhunting, Pony Club, eventing atmosphere, and he had even tried out for a place on the United States Olympic Three-Day Team. He had built several courses, beginning with his home course at the Essex Horse Trials, and had traveled to every important event in the 1970s to study course design and construction. Well before the competition he stated his intentions: "The boldest horse with the biggest jump or the greatest speed might not win, especially if the rider cannot make changes in line, speed, flexion, and frame during his round. Rider problems, forcing decisions and perhaps errors, will be stressed at Lexington, and the equestrian world will be watching to see if this approach achieves the 'correct' result: the best-prepared are the winners, the ill-prepared are the losers, but are not hurt . . ."

Obviously it was going to be a typical course of the seventies, technical and demanding, a rider course.

Haller carefully considered his previously-mentioned four essentials. The galloping track was laid out across a thousand acres of springy bluegrass turf, the closest America had to offer to the established sod of the great English parks. He spent hours in the placement of each single obstacle so that it would offer a true test; he took into account the caliber of horses that would be entered from the big names of England, Germany, and America and also considered the lesser-known contestants from the South American countries; and researched carefully to find native materials that would provide the solid, massive obstacles he needed for a true championship course. In all these things he succeeded admirably.

The fifth element, the climate, was of some concern because Kentucky can be hot and humid in the extreme. Although statistics showed that it was possible for the weather conditions to be suitable, anxiety persisted in the minds of experts.

The course Roger Haller came up with was admittedly big, but it was not too big for a World Championships. It asked a great many questions: there were complexes demanding big efforts not just at the beginning, or in the middle, or at the end, but all the way around. It had some innovative ideas and it was immaculate in its construction and in its attention to detail.

It followed the trend which had begun at Munich.

III
World Championships 1978

7

The Defender

*And if I should lose, let me stand by the road and
cheer as the winners go by*

BERTON BRALEY, "Prayer of a Sportsman"

I

Bruce read the newsletter giving details of the World Championships for
1978. "Hey, Carol!" he called. "Guess what? The dates for the competition fall on the same weekend in September that Burghley did. Do you
think that's an omen?"

The right to play host to the 1978 Championships belonged to America
because of Bruce's victory on Irish Cap in 1974. (It is the individual rather
than the team prize that counts in determining the ground for the next
match.) The competition had been awarded to Kentucky, which offered
more money than the other three states that had bid for the honor, and
the state planned to use the occasion to inaugurate its brand-new multi-
million-dollar Horse Park in Lexington.

Parts of Kentucky lie on a substrate of limestone left behind by a long-
forgotten seabed. The land is honeycombed with underground caves and
springs and the porous rock filters rainwater into sweet, pure reservoirs
that nourish the soil with rich minerals. The famous bluegrass that grows
as a result of this geological feature is ideal for the raising of horses.
Kentucky is renowned for its horses and its bourbon whiskey made with
the pure water, and for its Southern hospitality that markets both with
friendly enthusiasm. The countryside around Lexington is used almost
entirely for breeding farms that produce many of the world's greatest
Thoroughbred and Standardbred horses. Mile after mile of white or
creosoted board fences surround the rolling green fields and the large
barns that keep the flies off the elite of the American horse population.
Mares graze with their foals in the steamy heat, while the stallions, who
are also part of the tourist attraction, hold court to visiting mares from
all over the world.

Four miles to the north of the city, one of Lexington's oldest established
breeding farms, Walnut Hall, which was originally owned by a French
immigrant, covers 1,052 acres of this typical, rolling land. Its rich paddocks are shaded by huge walnut trees, and in the center there is a

OPPOSITE: Might Tango began his me-
teoric rise to fame by winning the Preliminary Three-Day Event at Blue
Ridge in 1978, thus amassing enough
points to force him into Advanced
competition at Ledyard and then at
Chesterland.

123

permanent steeplechase track. The largest barn in the world, 463 feet long by 60 feet wide, sits on a knoll overlooking the fields. The State of Kentucky bought Walnut Hall and spent $27 million on making it into their Horse Park — a showcase for their equine industry, and also a token of respect for the product.

II

Nobody seemed to mind the thousands of miles which separate Kentucky from most parts of the world. Competitors came from Australia, New Zealand, Japan, South America, Europe, England, Ireland, Canada, and, of course, from all over America. The script called for a repeat performance from the defending champions, Bruce Davidson and Irish Cap, and the victorious American team, under the stage direction of Jack LeGoff.

There were new faces among the American cast, and new horses. Of the original team members, only Bruce and Mike Plumb remained.

LeGoff seriously considers Might Tango as a prospect for Kentucky after his dazzling performance at Chesterland in July 1978.

All that silver becomes a problem to hold. Mike Plumb and Better and Better after winning the Advanced Division at Blue Ridge 1978.

Officiating is serious business. General F. F. Wing and Mrs. I. Presnikoff intent on the stadium jumping phase, with the indefatigable Eileen Thomas recording the scores.

Denny Emerson was there, but as assistant coach because his horses had gone lame. Don Sachey had retired from competition and was coaching privately. As the host nation, America had the right to enter not only the four official team riders and the two individuals that were allowed to all countries, but also an additional six individual riders. Under the generalship of LeGoff they seemed like a small army.

Earlier in the year, LeGoff had pointed out that some of the team horses were reaching the upper age limits for competition. "They are stepping on their beards," he said, with his customary flair for language. "We have to be careful with them." Both Irish Cap and Bally Cor, the Olympic gold-medal-winning mare, were showing their age, and for this reason, they were campaigned very lightly during that spring and summer. Bruce had saved Irish Cap for the late summer and had won the selection trial at Ledyard Farm in July with authority. It seemed as if Irish Cap was in his old form and would defend his title in Kentucky.

Meanwhile, Might Tango, the ugly duckling, had been improving steadily. He had won the Preliminary Championships in 1977, and Bruce had upgraded him to Intermediate level in the spring of 1978 in the hope that the horse would reach his best in time for the 1980 Olympic Games in Moscow. After winning the Preliminary three-day event at Blue Ridge, Bruce entered Might Tango for the Open division at Ledyard to test the horse's ability over the formidable course fences which had been tailored especially for the selection trials. Tango met the challenge superbly. The complex fences seemed to wake him up for the first time, and he paid attention to what he was doing. Bruce had an electric thrill when the big gray cantered down to the notorious Coffin jump at Ledyard and skipped through it with ease. "This is really a fancy horse," he said afterwards. "He's really grown up this winter and settled down. He'll be something to watch in two years' time."

Chesterland Farm itself was the site of the final selection trials for the Americans. Bruce's ambition had long been to hold a first-class three-day event in his beloved Chester County, with its undulating hills and open spaces. He had designed a big, straightforward galloping course, a course for the real three-day horse.

Mixed in with Bruce's delight over the Chesterland Trials was his concern for Irish Cap. After Ledyard the big horse had seemed to lose some of his elasticity. Unwilling though he was to consider an alternative mount for the Championships, in the back of Bruce's mind was the thought that perhaps, just perhaps, Might Tango might be ready if he needed a substitute.

On the day of the Chesterland Trials, Might Tango came out of his stable and looked with surprise at the crowds of people in his backyard. His ears pricked, and he strutted around the warm-up area as if he owned the place, which in effect he did. When Bruce rode him into the arena, the big gray pointed his toes and showed off for the judges. He won the dressage phase with a score of 39.6 penalties. Irish Cap, slightly stiff in his hind legs, scored 51.3.

The weather, hot and humid as it had been throughout the summer, threatened thunderstorms all day, and LeGoff, concerned about his team horses, ordered all the possible candidates to hold back on their speeds.

Might Tango sometimes spent more time on two legs than on four. Here he is objecting to being left behind when the other horses are returning to the barn, but it is in a spirit of play.

127

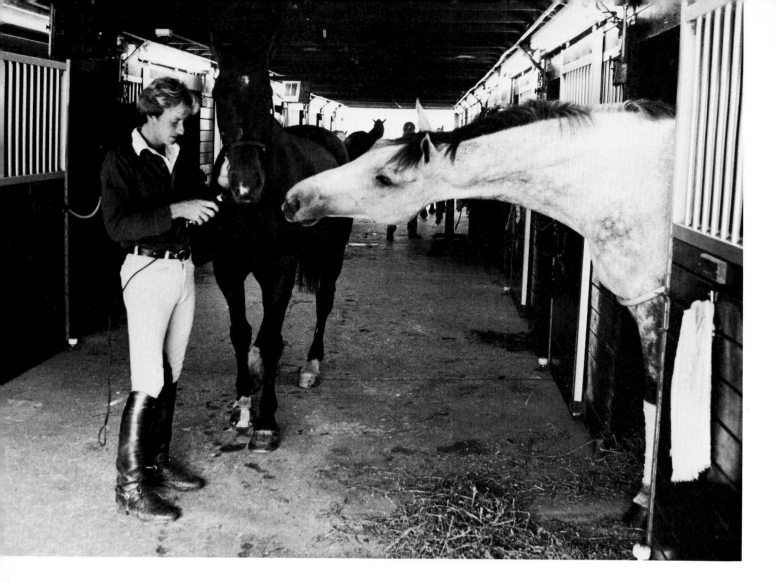

Might Tango is intensely jealous of any attention paid to another horse. Here he vies for attention as Bruce clips Irish Cap's whiskers.

"We don't want to lose the competition in Kentucky right here," he explained. Bruce kept Irish Cap under firm control; but having nothing to lose on the young Might Tango, because he was not thought ready for the Championships, he let the horse go along at his own speed. Might Tango's own speed is a very fast one indeed. He galloped easily over the big fences, jumping in better style than ever before to win the Advanced division. "That horse can certainly gallop," said Mike Plumb, who was still sitting on the sidelines after an injury at Ledyard and hoping to recover in time for Lexington.

When the World short list was read out that evening, Irish Cap was announced as Bruce's first horse. All the riders who had been chosen for the trip to Kentucky remained at Chesterland thereafter for the final training period with LeGoff. The horses were stabled in the hunt stables opposite the driveway leading up to Chesterland Farm, and each day the riders brought them out one by one to jog in front of LeGoff for a check on their soundness.

A week later Irish Cap went lame, and Bruce discussed with LeGoff the possibility of substituting Might Tango. This was a bitter blow for both coach and rider, as they wanted to rely on Irish Cap for the upcoming Championships; they both knew that there were still many question marks about the temperamental, inexperienced Might Tango, who was only seven years old.

Once again, Bruce was under the coach's orders; but now there were great differences in their relationship. Bruce was no longer the eager novice under complete control. He had been out on his own for four years and had succeeded, both as a competitor and as a trainer of horses and riders. He was glad to be part of the team again and was anxious for the instruction, but this time he had the added pressure of being defending world champion and a rider of established reputation.

LeGoff had changed, too. His successes with American riders had been incredible. Having won the World Championships, the Pan-American Games, and the Olympic Games, he was established as the finest coach in the world. He had mellowed, becoming less military. His English was almost perfect and he no longer struggled to express himself; to the dismay of the younger riders he could now be scathing in English as well as in French. His un-American training methods had been accepted by some of the diehard older riders who had been established before he arrived in America, in proof of which Jim Wofford had returned to the team with his new acquisition, Carawich, happy to work with the coach after a long period during which he had been unable to produce a horse for the top competitions.

Though Irish Cap and Might Tango had never been able to get along together, a curious thing happened when Irish Cap went lame: Might Tango accepted him as a friend. "It's uncanny," Bruce said to Jane. "Before, you couldn't even lead them out together, and *now* look at them." In Jane's view, the new tolerance had come about because Might Tango understood that the reigning World Champion was no longer a threat to him.

Yet in all other ways their attitudes remained the same. While Irish Cap welcomed visitors to the stables, graciously consenting to be patted, Might Tango grabbed at people's clothes, demanded attention, and then nipped them in the rear as they walked away. "He's a brat. He doesn't like anyone except Jane and me and Buck," Bruce said, amused. Buck, Bruce's young son, wandered in and out of the big horse's stall without a trace of fear, and Might Tango watched him carefully as he toddled about the aisle with his red and yellow fire engine.

III

The horses for the Championships were packed up at night and driven to Kentucky in the dark to avoid the heat. The trip took fourteen hours.

The riders flew down together in a group, as if they were a bunch of kids going off to summer camp. It was a warm, friendly time, and though the older riders tended to be quiet, the younger ones laughed and joked. They had a feeling of closeness after having worked hard together for the past three and a half weeks.

Bruce faced the big barn in the Horse Park with awe. "It's so different from those little tent stalls at Burghley," he thought. Might Tango had a huge box stall just inside the main entrance to the stable, with room

Sometimes the life of a champion is deadly dull.

enough for two horses his size. Jane settled him down into a bed of deep shavings and made sure that he had plenty of cold, fresh water. The oppressive heat of the long summer hung chokingly over the Horse Park, and the European horses, unacclimatized, stood listlessly in their stalls, dripping sweat. Their grooms sent out for electric fans to stir up the heavy air.

When Kentucky was first announced as the site for the competition, several people had sharply questioned the advisability of holding a three-day event there at such a hot time of year. In answer, Kentucky public relations people had come up with statistics for the month of September showing that, despite an average temperature in the high seventies and the low eighties, the humidity would be low and the air would be fresh enough to ride in. No one thought to remind the public relations department of the story about the statistician who drowned in a stream with an average depth of three and a half feet.

By the time the Americans arrived, almost all the other competitors and their horses were already installed. Bruce and Carol greeted old friends and introduced Buck, who had made the trip with them. Nearly everyone wanted to inspect their rivals. Lucinda Prior-Palmer, who, since Burghley, had been European Champion twice running, invited Bruce to see Village Gossip, her new horse. She took off his sheet to show him off, telling Bruce all about his bad habits and his good habits, and about how very fast he was, and what she thought of him. She showed him her other horse, Killaire, and took him on a conducted tour of all the English horses and told him how each was going. In return, Bruce introduced her to the American horses and riders and took her to see Might Tango. Lucinda said, with understanding, how sorry she was to hear that Irish Cap had been left behind.

All the teams were stabled under the same roof, the riders ambling informally through each other's sections, in contrast to Burghley, where the rain and the arrangement of the stabling had made casual socializing difficult. Bruce came in for a lot of good-natured teasing because the official program had his photo on the cover. But the horse in the photo was not Irish Cap, it was Might Tango, in the water jump at Chesterland. "Perhaps this is another omen," thought Bruce.

Kentucky outdid itself in welcome. No one could fault the hospitality, except to say that perhaps there was too much of it. Invitations showered down on the riders and their associates: "The Mayor requests . . ." "The

Lucinda Prior-Palmer enjoys a quiet moment with Village Gossip. Like Bruce, and all event riders, she has a deep affection for her horses.

RIGHT: Liz Ashton and Sunrise have competed for Canada not only in Three-Day but on their international Open Jumping Team. The Canadians, because of their severe winters, frequently compete in U.S. events, as above at Chesterland 1979.

The grave responsibility of the judges has moments of lightness. Colonel Anton Buehler, Colonel Donald W. Thackeray, and Lt. Colonel Frank Weldon share a smile.

American Horse Shows Association requests . . ." "Mr. and Mrs. So-and-so request . . ." With parties every night, competitors were frantic to get all their preparations completed. They had to ride their horses, often getting up at 4:30 A.M. to avoid the heat of the day; they had to walk and study the course and get ready to compete. Often they finished all this at 10:00 P.M., only to be faced with the prospect of having to go out and socialize. The social life was so insistent that the Americans established a roster. Each night four different riders went to represent the home side, leaving the others free to get on with their work.

It was a killing schedule, and the heat did not help. Bruce, who thrives on hot weather, was not affected, but the Europeans found the constant muggy atmosphere debilitating and from the beginning of the week they lobbied for the cross-country phase to be started early in the morning to escape the worst of the heat. But the officials were adamant: the time schedule must remain as published.

All the competitors, their coaches, and the liaison officers assigned to each team were billeted at the same hotel, making a big, friendly group. The "Kiwis," the New Zealanders who had raised the funds for their trip themselves because they had no national society to assist them, held a birthday dinner for their coach. Jack LeGoff and Denny Emerson stopped by the table to wish him happy birthday and were joined by the Argentine team, who, speaking little English, sang "Happy Birthday" in Spanish.

IV

The official inspection of the cross-country course took place on the Tuesday before the competition began. The initial reaction was that while the course was beautifully conceived and built with precision and a fanatic

Roger Haller, the course designer, and Wolfgang Feld, the Technical Delegate appointed by the FEI, discuss their responsibilities in Lexington, Kentucky.

attention to detail, it was exceptionally large. LeGoff, who has seen perhaps every major course in the world, said it was the biggest he had ever seen.

The steeplechase course, set around the track of the permanent 'chase course, differed sharply from the standard steeplechase used for three-day eventing. It contained several different types of fences, and, in contrast to the flat land that is normally chosen for such courses, it was built on rolling ground much like the hills at Chesterland. Bruce walked it with the others. "This is too small," he thought as they started out; and then suddenly, "Holy Jesus! This is not small, it's enormous!"

When he had finished his inspection he was empty-minded, experience warning him not to decide, "This will be easy" or "This is too big, too different." Instead he thought, "I'm going to have to walk this several times and study it and learn it. It isn't going to ride like a 'chase course, it's going to ride more like a cross-country course. It's not a course that you can ask a horse to run over, but one that wants a horse who makes time naturally. It's like the ground at home."

The American riders walked along with their coach, listening to his reactions to the fences. They knew they had several more days ahead in which to study the fences and the line to take.

Bruce worried also about his horse, who was fretting in his stall. For the first two days Might Tango had enjoyed the new surroundings, but, unlike Irish Cap, he hated crowds. His stall was next to the stable entrance, and as he was an unknown quantity and belonged to the World Champion he came in for a great deal of attention. People peering in at him and poking him around and moving him so that they could take a good look at him drove him crazy. He started to walk back and forth in his stall, refusing to eat or drink. Trying desperately to coax him out of his sulk, Jane decided that he needed a toy; so, borrowing a car, she

The study and measuring of the cross-country course occupies much of a coach's time. Colonel Bill Lithgow of Great Britain pauses in his task of measuring exact distances to talk with Jack LeGoff during his inspection of a fence.

drove into town and came back with a red-and-yellow plastic duck to put into his water bucket. Might Tango was enchanted. He spent hours playing with his duck, bobbing it up and down in the water with his nose.

As Bruce went over the cross-country course he tried to analyze it from the point of view of his young horse. With Irish Cap he would have known exactly what to do at each fence, but Might Tango had never seen anything to equal these fences and Bruce was still not sure how the horse would react. He looked at Fence 3, the Park Pavilion: two big benches covered by a roof. "It's not the roof I have to worry about," he thought. "It's the approach: I have to worry about the crowds. The horse will come straight toward the crowds, turn away from them, and in three strides he'll have to jump from the light into the dark. This is where he will make his first mistake. He's never seen anything like this and I strongly suspect he's going to hit it hard. I have to be sure he doesn't lose his confidence. If he hits it as I expect and stays on his feet, then it will serve to wake him up and it will be good for him."

Fences 8 and 9 were listed in the program as the Sinkhole; a nasty vertical fence before a natural ditch that offered no real landing. The Americans rechristened it "the Stinkhole." The quickest way through lay on the right, but LeGoff advised his riders to take a longer, slower route on the left-hand side and up through the middle. Bruce agreed that with Might Tango, he should play safe and jump the longer route.

Walking on, the band of riders came to the complex called Old Fort Lexington because it was a replica of forts built on America's frontiers. A cluster of log cabins, complete with a cooking pot hanging on a tripod, led to a central bank protected by a moat and topped with a stockade. Mary Hazzard, one of the American riders and Bruce's friend and neighbor from Pennsylvania, climbed to the top of the central bank. "Wow!" she gasped. "There's only one way to ride this. You'll have to gallop down to it as if three thousand Indians were really after you and you just gotta get through those gates before they close!"

The most artistic fences were grouped around the lake, which came just over halfway on a long, tiring course. Bruce knew that his horse would need help to get through the water.

Yet the real killer was still to come: as the group looked down the hill towards the Serpent (Fences 23, 24, and 25), Bruce thought, "This is a big complex," and he got out his map to get a feel for what was waiting at the bottom of the slope. "This is really ingenious," he thought as he stood looking at it, trying to find a straight line through the three zigzags. "I think the first part is jumpable and the second part shouldn't give us much trouble; but I don't like the third part at all. I don't see *any* way through that looks nice. This is obviously going to be a fence we spend hours trying to figure out."

The only other obstacle that bothered him was the Maze (Fences 29, 30, and 31). It was late in the course, and he was not sure just how much horse he would have left at this point. On Irish Cap he knew how he would approach it, because he knew he could control the speed. With Might Tango he did not know, and could not estimate, how quick the horse would be or how he would react to the closely set brush obstacles and the sharply angled turns.

The "mini-moke" of Lady Hugh Russell serves as a rallying point for Lord Hugh Russell, one of the mainstays of the British contingent, and Roger Haller on the day of the course unveiling.

LEFT: On the way to yet another press interview, LeGoff courteously answers the questions of a young fan.

135

Driving Carol and Buck back to the hotel, Bruce brooded about the course. It was very big and very demanding — probably more demanding than Burghley had been. He hoped he could get around it on his "baby." A great many people were doubtful that Might Tango was a world class horse because of his temperament, and most thought that it was much too early for this seven-year-old to be competing at the top level. Suddenly, the confidence that he had felt in Irish Cap came back to the young rider, strengthening his determination to prove to the world that his new horse was a champion. "There is no point in coming all this way with the young horse unless I decide to do it in style," he thought.

V

The first casualty happened before the competition even began. Power Game, one of the German horses, was tied to a washpipe getting a final bath when he reared back, tore the pipe from the ground, and galloped off with the clattering piece of metal dragging from his lead rope. He fell several times in his terror-stricken flight and broke a small splint bone in one front leg before he was caught.

This accident made the German entry one horse short — only five could now compete instead of the permitted six. The British, the Canadians, and the Americans had all brought alternative mounts, and the Germans, who had thought that no spare horses were allowed, were understandably upset when they discovered that they could have done the same.

Violent thunderstorms were forecast for the morning of the veterinary inspection; so severe that Kentucky state troopers circulated through the barns with the warning to keep all equipment under cover. Grooms were busily braiding manes and brushing off specks of dust that had settled on their horses' coats, preparing them for their first official appearance.

Bruce watched Jane rub up Might Tango's sleek coat until the iron-gray dapples reflected the light. The horse looked ready to run — full of hard, firm flesh and stronger than he had ever seemed before. The skinny, upside-down neck had filled out with muscles and the huge head no longer looked out of proportion to the rest of the big frame. He splashed his duck around his water bucket, impatient to be off.

Just as the first horses were led from the stable the sultry black clouds overhead opened up. Rain poured down in such sheets that the veterinarians, the officials, the grooms and their horses, and most of the crowd fled for the shelter of the barn. Since it looked as if the storm would be prolonged, a decision to vet the horses indoors was made by the Ground Jury. The inspection panel arranged themselves at one end of the barn, and the horses were jogged down the aisle towards them. Might Tango was frantic; he hated crowds, and when the mass of people came rushing in past his stall with their umbrellas and raincoats and ponchos flapping in the stormy wind, he went crazy. Bruce and Jane tried to lead him quietly around with the other horses, who were parading equally at the far end of the stables, but he would not settle. He plunged and reared, crashing indiscriminately into the sides of the barn and into people.

Afraid that someone would be injured, Bruce led his horse outside,

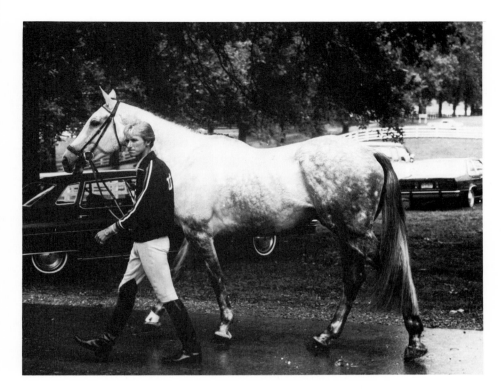

Might Tango was upset by the crowds inside the barn at the vet check so Bruce took him outside and walked him in the rain.

where it had almost stopped raining, and walked him up and down to calm him. Might Tango settled and passed the veterinary inspection, jogging in front of the panel, looking out of the corner of his eye at the crowds squashed into the small area, and showing off his long reaching stride.

VI

The pressures on LeGoff were greater than those on any one of his riders. He had to name four horses and riders to the official team, and he was in a very awkward position. The choices facing him were these: Mike Plumb, the most experienced rider, also had the most experienced horse in Laurenson, but Mike was only just back in the saddle after a serious injury and might not be fit enough. Tad Coffin was the defending Olympic Champion, but game old Bally Cor had soundness problems. Jim Wofford on Carawich had been going very well, and Jim had the experience of many international competitions behind him. Bruce was the defending champion, but he had a very green, untried horse. Mary Anne Tauskey and little Marcus Aurelius had been going well all year. Caroline Treviranus had been plagued by accidents, though her horse, Comic Relief, was sound and well. Torrance Watkins had done well with Red's Door, but it was the first time in international competition for both. The other riders were short on experience and had very varied horses.

The ultimate decision is the responsibility of the coach. If he guesses wrong he gets the blame, and if he guesses right he gets the glory. Jack LeGoff decided to go with his most experienced riders: Bruce, Mike, Jim, and Tad. Mary Anne and Torrance were the two individual riders, and the others rode as the extra six allowed. LeGoff told Bruce he must go first, since they were unsure of Might Tango.

Bruce's first reaction was "Why me?" But, as he thought about the order of go, he realized that this would give him an advantage. He believed his horse to be the fastest in the competition, so that if he could go clean and well he would at once prove his point and would put pressure on the competitors following after. "This is good," he thought. "This is right where I want to be. I want to go early."

The draw for the team order put the Americans in fifth. The order of play is that one rider from each team starts until a member from every country has performed. Then some of the individual riders are fitted into the lineup, then the block of second riders from each team, then more individuals, and so on. As the first American competitor, Bruce would wear the number 5.

While all this was being decided, over 450 representatives of the media had converged on Kentucky to cover the event. All of them wanted an interview with the World Champion. Bruce was short on time and tried to avoid as many interviews as he could. The extra pressure of being a famous rider began to wear on him. One persistent reporter caught up with him as he was going out to walk the 4¾-mile course for a third time.

"The dressage phase starts tomorrow," began the reporter. "Dressage is often compared to figure skating. Which world figure skater would you compare Might Tango with?"

Bruce looked at him in amazement. "I know nothing about figure

Might Tango's dressage test.

OPPOSITE: The bronze medallists Helmut Rethemeier and Ladalco in the dressage arena in Kentucky.

skating," he answered. "I know none of the figure skaters. Anyway, Might Tango would never be a figure skater — he's more like an ice hockey player!"

The Dressage Test

On Thursday morning Bruce dressed with care, sticking to his routine of doing everything by the left first. He wore the same breeches, the same boots, the same hat (a little sunburned now), and the same red coat with the white piping and blue collar that he had worn at Burghley four years before. Might Tango was braided and polished, shiny as only Jane could make him. Bruce rode him round to the warm-up arena in back of the grandstands.

There were amazing numbers of spectators: over 13,500 people came for that first day of dressage, which was almost unheard of in U.S. eventing. Most of them wore raincoats or had brought along their rain ponchos in case the threatening clouds opened up again. They were a knowledgeable audience, sitting quietly while each horse performed and applauding only when the test had been completed.

Might Tango looked at the crowds nervously out of the corners of his eyes and refused to concentrate. "This is not going to be anything like Burghley," thought Bruce. "I'm going to be lucky to keep him in one piece. I'd give anything for another week or even just another day to settle him down."

As Bruce moved from one warm-up area to the next, getting progressively closer to the grandstand as his time approached, he tried to

keep his horse active but calm. Might Tango was, in fact, electric: he thought he was back at the racetrack.

When the starting bell rang, Bruce took a deep breath, Might Tango moved out at the canter, and they entered the arena, moving up the centerline for the first salute. Might Tango quivered but stood still. Bruce moved him onwards in the trot, concentrating on each precious second as the test proceeded. Might Tango kept trying to drop the bit and look sideways at the crowds, but Bruce encouraged him forward, keeping the rhythm. "This isn't what this horse is capable of doing," he thought, "but at least he is behaving and being precise. I can sacrifice his brilliance for a steady test this time." When the scores were posted Might Tango had a total penalty score of 61.4, which placed him among the leaders at the end of the day. Young Story Jenks, one of Bruce's students from Pennsylvania, took the overnight lead on Toughkenamon with a score of 57.0. Bruce was delighted.

The drama had begun, and was going, in the view of knowledgeable international event followers, according to script. The Americans, British, and Germans were the teams most highly regarded to win, while all the rest were outsiders. The individual competition looked as if it would be between Mike Plumb of the United States on Laurenson, and the Badminton winner, Jane Holderness-Roddam on Warrior who was two

Joanne Bridgman from New Zealand on Bandolier. The "Kiwis" had never before competed in international three-day eventing, and had raised most of the money for the long trip by themselves. Because of the lack of funds, and also their stringent quarantine regulations, they were forced to sell off all their horses before returning home. Bandolier was purchased for Lucinda Prior-Palmer of Great Britain.

OPPOSITE: Regulations state that all riders must come up to the required 165 pounds for both the speed and endurance phases and the stadium jumping. Bruce weighs in with his saddle.

points behind. Though no one knew much about Might Tango, they respected Bruce as a formidable competitor. The young New Zealanders were not expected to have much chance because it was their first appearance in international eventing, and Topic, supposedly one of their best horses, placed last of all in the dressage.

At the end of the second day the script still had no surprises to offer. The United States was the leader, one point ahead of Germany, and Great Britain was nine points away in third. Mike Plumb on Laurenson had taken the individual lead and Jane Holderness-Roddam was second. Pundits nodded their heads: the form was right.

Might Tango finished the dressage in eleventh place.

Bruce woke early on the morning of cross-country. Starting, of course, with the left arm first, he slipped on a short-sleeved, navy blue shirt that Carol had bought earlier in the week and that he had already worn so it would not be new on performance day. Superstition dictates that riders never wear anything brand-new for a competition.

Speed and Endurance

He drove out to the Horse Park for one last walk around the course, checking the problem fences. LeGoff was there early also and they went together for a final look at the Maze. Bruce explained to LeGoff how he planned to take it; but LeGoff pointed out an alternate approach, and as he studied the fence and thought about Might Tango, Bruce realized that the coach's idea was the better one. Mike Plumb arrived, and he and Bruce inspected the footing at the Jenny Lane Crossing, where the road had been covered with tanbark.

Trying to kill time, Bruce walked slowly back to the stables. Once again the waiting was getting on his nerves.

Might Tango was nearly ready and Jane was working with the galloping boots that would protect his front and back legs against bruising if he hit a jump. She had laid out the bridle with the gag snaffle bit, which gave Bruce an added control over the impetuous gray, and she had Bruce's saddle ready.

Bruce put strips of adhesive tape on his left arm and on them wrote down the distances and speeds of the four separate phases so that he would have a quick reference as he was galloping along. He picked up his crash helmet with the dark blue cover and red and white stripes and USA on the front and, taking his saddle, strolled off to the official scales. Jane led Might Tango down behind him.

It was 10 A.M., and the first horse had just left on Phase A of the roads and tracks. Bruce weighed in, saddled Might Tango, and rode over to wait by the starter. At 10:20 A.M. he was given the signal to start.

Might Tango's restless energy had not been dampened by the weather. He did an extended trot for most of the 6,000 meters (about 3¾ miles) leading to the steeplechase course. It was relatively cool that morning with a thin cloud cover holding off the burning rays of the sun, but the humidity was high. As soon as the cloud cover wore off it promised to be another scorching day.

The steeplechase course was long — 3,795 meters (2⅓ miles) — and it had to be covered at a speed of 690 meters per minute, which was extremely fast. Yet, while it was exactly the same distance as the Burghley

Bruce on Might Tango on the steeple-chase course in Kentucky.

OPPOSITE: On the steeplechase after Might Tango had settled into his stride.

steeplechase had been, the course in Kentucky was twice as difficult because of the undulating ground and the variation in the fences. It was not a simple course of brush fences which could be taken easily.

Once again, Lucinda was riding ahead of Bruce, and when he reached the steeplechase course he learned from LeGoff, who was at the start, that she had gone round in incredibly fast time.

Coming out of the starting box, Bruce took a firm hold on Might Tango. He went deliberately slowly over the first two fences, giving his horse a chance to feel out the course. The third fence was rather small, a birch rail with brush sticking up and water behind it. The grass, still wet with a heavy condensation of morning dew, was dangerously slip-pery. Might Tango tried to chip in a short stride on the approach to the third fence, slid about fifteen feet towards it with his hind legs starting to do the splits, and somehow launched himself into the air and landed on his hind legs first. He scared himself badly.

At the next fence, a small bank with a hedge on the top, Bruce felt Might Tango slowing up and knew that the horse had learned from his acrobatics at the fence before and was now being cautious, not wanting to commit himself to jumping out of a bold stride.

Two fences after that there was a bullfinch — a high hedge that the horses had to jump through rather than over — and Bruce was not taking any chances with this one. He rode Might Tango firmly into it, and the horse left out a stride and dove feet first into the brush. Bruce sat quietly, holding the reins and trying to balance the horse so that he would be reassured and encouraged to settle, and the rest of the course went by quickly as Might Tango's confidence grew. At the end, Bruce dismounted and led him for the first few minutes on the roads and tracks of Phase C to give them both time to recover.

Under pressure from worried experts, who felt that the speed and endurance course was too severe in view of the heat and humidity, the Ground Jury had made a token concession on Phase C and had shortened the distance by three-quarters of a mile. Since the time allowance remained the same, the riders were thereby given an extra five minutes to help their horses recover from the exertions of the steeplechase, but nevertheless there were still more than six miles of roads and tracks to endure before the vet box was reached.

As Bruce and Might Tango trotted quietly into the vet box they were met by a badly worried coach. No one had yet completed the awesome cross-country course: the first two horses had had to be retired and neither of the second two had yet come home, so LeGoff not only had no information about how the course was riding but had good reason to feel uneasy.

"He didn't jump too well on the steeplechase," he said, referring to Might Tango.

"I know."

"Take your time. Don't hurry things on the cross-country."

Bruce said teasingly, "Are you nervous?"

"Damn right I'm nervous," replied the coach.

"Don't be," said Bruce. "We'll be all right. He jumped badly on the steeplechase because he was slipping, which maybe you couldn't see. But he *did* get himself together, and he *did* jump nicely at the end. Once we get by Fence Three we'll see you shortly thereafter."

Might Tango took the first two fences with ease, but as Bruce swung him down towards the Park Pavilion he pricked his ears and focused on the people who bulged the ropes on the left of the obstacle. Bruce turned him away from the crowd and in toward the Pavilion. Might Tango

Might Tango over the approach to
Fort Lexington, Fence 13. "I never
thought he'd step on it."

Might Tango is well in hand coming
down off Fort Lexington.

Out over the final element of Fort
Lexington.

gawked at it, hung a front leg on the top, and scrambled into the dark interior. Once in, he took three microscopic strides, in a space where there was only room for two, and jumped neatly out over the other side.

"I *knew* he would take three strides in there," thought Bruce. "Sometimes he's just like a little eleven-hand pony. He can fold those great long legs up like no other horse." He gave Tango a pat on the neck, grateful to be through.

Bruce's whole concentration was on his horse and on the course. He wasn't thinking, "I know Lucinda is going to be very fast," or, "I would like to beat Mike Plumb," but only, "I want to ride this horse to the best of my ability. I want him to go around this course better than he has ever gone. I am going to let him run as much as he wants, but I am not going to risk a clear round by going too fast — I don't feel the need to prove he is the fastest horse. I want him to jump this course clear and he'll still be hard to catch."

Might Tango was steady on the bit, which was very unlike him; he was light and responsive, not pulling like his usual aggressive self, and his easy gallop reminded Bruce of Irish Cap at Burghley. Bruce decided just to let him cruise and not to ask for anything more in case it wasn't there. Coming up to the Sinkhole he chose the safer left-handed approach — and then felt like a fool when the big horse made nothing of it.

They came to the daunting Fort Lexington complex with the horse moving surely in his stride. Unexpectedly, Might Tango banked the shed of the easy approach jump (Fence 13), and the shock of the abrupt slackening of pace threw Bruce forward onto his horse's neck. "I never thought he'd step on it," he said afterwards. "He just jumped up on top of it and crawled off and I was sitting up in front of the saddle before the big Fort Lexington bank thinking, 'Holy mackerel, this is not exactly where I planned to be.' And then I just kicked on like crazy, and he left out a stride and jumped almost to the top of the bank.

"There was no way you could scramble through the stuff on top nicely; you just jumped in and out, not thinking about the striding. The horse had to just scrabble through and trip over the out as best he could. You *had* to make your horse trip over the out. Then you went down and jumped over a little feed trough just like the sheds on the approach side, and that was purely a control thing to make sure the riders kept their heads about them once they landed."

They came halfway, to the Head of the Lake complex. Might Tango jumped up and off the first bank. Bruce felt they had to bounce off the bank; everyone talked about jumping on the bank and putting in a short stride, but how can you put in a short stride in nine feet? Tango did exactly as anticipated: he bounced nimbly off the bank into the water, and Bruce kept him down to a trot through the lake to reduce the drag effect from the depth of the water. He jumped up the big out-bank and cantered on up over the birch rails. The noise of the thousands who watched his quality was left behind in the speed of his going.

As he came into the Serpent, Bruce looked for his line. He noticed the abnormally big crowds and wondered if they were waiting for him to make a mistake. "This horse has five legs. He won't fall," he thought. He had no inkling of the trouble to be caused by this complex, intent

For the first time in America, the crowds at the World Championships rivalled or exceeded those in England at a three-day event.

only on riding from A to B to C and on, doing his homework the whole way round. Might Tango hit the last part of the Serpent, catching one hind leg on it and twisting badly in mid air, but he put a front leg down and recovered.

You are conscious of the crowd in eventing. You can hear their sound when you slow up to set your horse right before a fence, and their chatter of approval or dislike as you ride through. The groundswell that broke on Might Tango's recovery came as a surprise to Bruce: he didn't know that only one of the four horses who had started out before him had got as far as the Serpent, or that that one, Lucinda Prior-Palmer's Village Gossip, had fallen there.

Coming down to the last fence on the course, Might Tango pricked his ears, made a smooth jump, and galloped on down to the finish line. Bruce pulled him up to a slow canter, patting him and praising him for his efforts. He trotted him up to the scales, dismounted, dropped his whip, undid the girth and pulled the saddle off. He stepped onto the scales and waited while the officials recorded his weight, stepped down, patted Tango on the neck, put down his saddle, and turned to meet LeGoff. Jane led the horse away to the buckets of water she had put ready for him in the shade.

Quickly, LeGoff asked how the course had ridden. He needed this vital information to pass along to the other American riders. He told Bruce that despite Lucinda's fall at the Serpent, she had still finished incredibly fast.

As they stood there running over the problems of the course, Bruce felt a tap on his shoulder. Marty Simensen, the team veterinarian, was right behind him. "Bruce, you'd better give us a hand with Might Tango if you and Jack have finished," he said.

Bruce looked across at his horse: Might Tango was staggering as if he were drunk, swaying back and forth with buckling knees. In his intense nervous excitement he had run to the very end of his strength. The heat and the humidity had been too much, and his natural air conditioning, the body's ability to dissipate heat, had shut off, sending the blood to his brain. His temperature was dangerously high. He was unable to walk — could barely even stand — and could have collapsed.

There was no time for hesitation. Marty Simensen snapped at anyone in hearing distance, "Get ice. Get towels. You hustle. You do it *right now*. I don't care who you are or what your name is — MOVE!" He organized a rescue team. He knew exactly what had to be done, and without his swift efficiency Might Tango might well have collapsed altogether.

Nightmare

The immediate need was to get the horse's temperature down. Bruce held his head and someone else held his tail to hold him up, while people on each side of him worked feverishly to keep him soaked with water and ice. Ice water was applied to all the major veins, iced towels were held on the vital spots, and intravenous injections of fluids, electrolytes, glucose, and phenylbutazone were pumped into his system. He was taking short, shallow breaths that did not carry oxygen into his lungs, so an oxygen tank was brought up and his nostrils were enclosed with a breathing tube.

Gulping oxygen, Might Tango stood with muscles quivering and legs shaking. No one looked at a watch or had time to ask how others were doing on the course. All their attention and energy was concentrated on the young horse who had given every bit of his strength and his courage.

It seemed a long time, but actually it was only minutes before his temperature began to drop. Bruce poured ice water onto his horse, moved him forward a few steps, and poured more water on him. Marty Simensen kept the intravenous fluids running into the jugular vein in the neck, keeping a close watch on the horse's vital signs and explaining to Bruce exactly what could happen and what signs to look for. Bruce had tremendous faith in the veterinarian and was immensely thankful that the finest medical help had been right on hand at the end of the course.

Once his temperature had dropped the horse began to recover. His pulse rate lowered, and his breathing became easier. Jane was able to walk him very slowly back to the stables.

As soon as his horse was out of danger, Bruce had to turn his attention back to the competition and the other riders. It was part of his job to tell each of the Americans how the fences had ridden and advise them on what to do to make their round better and safer. LeGoff was more and more disturbed by the reports coming in from riders and onlookers; disasters were happening out on the course at an unheard-of rate. The heat had increased, and by the time the horses came into the vet box, after Phase C and before the cross-country, they were already more tired than usual.

Horse after horse fell on the grueling four and three-quarter miles of cross-country. Jim Wofford and Carawich turned over at the Serpent; Tad Coffin and Bally Cor fell not once but twice. Jane Holderness-Roddam fell twice, and she and Chris Collins, also from England, were

Bruce Davidson (USA) on Might Tango at the Serpent.

1. As we come into the first element I am trying to hit it with as much momentum as possible. It was downhill to the first part, and I tried for as much energy as possible to carry us through the complex. At the moment of take-off, Tango is amazed by the big ditch and is having a good look as he prepares to jump.

2, 3. He makes a big jump safely over the first part.

4. He is an amazing horse for his size. He has the agility and balance needed to make a sharp turn like this one towards the second element.

5. Here I can see the stride for the second jump and start to make a positive aggressive move.

6. The crucial moment on the second element was the approach to the take-off point. The horse had to be able to use his head and neck in order to see where to place his feet, otherwise there was the danger of taking off from the top of the knoll instead of putting in one more stride.

7. Here we meet the correct take-off point.

8, 9. Tango shows the tremendous scope and power left in him on the tail end of the course.

10. He lands between the arms of the V shape of the fence.

2 3

5 4

8 7

Continued overleaf.

149

14

17 **16**

12   **11**

13

11. Again Might Tango makes a quick recovery and is able to make a balanced turn towards the final jump. It was important to turn away from the line of the course so as to jump straight out over one of the points formed in the fence, as this gave as clear a ground line as possible.

12. As in the second element, the horse needed to use his head and neck to size up the situation. I did not deprive Tango of the opportunity to do this.

13. We hit the spot I wanted.

14. Tango catches his left leg causing him to twist severely.

15

15. But at the moment of landing he shows his uncanny ability to recover his balance.

16. He gets himself back on course . . .

17. . . . and continues.

eliminated. Herbert Blocker on Albrant for Germany had retired at the Serpent.

The American list, of course, was of most interest to LeGoff. As the afternoon wore on he learned that Mary Anne Tauskey and her little horse Marcus Aurelius (nicknamed the "bionic pony") had had one refusal but had finished the course, that Caroline Treviranus had also had a stop but finished, that Torrance Watkins and Red's Door had fallen at the Serpent, that Desiree Smith and Foxie had retired there, that Ralph Hill and Sergeant Gilbert had gone around the course clean, and that Mary Hazzard, who never expected to make the list of American riders in the first place, had chosen to hack slowly around the course and had finished with no faults but lots of time penalties. Mike Huber and Gold Chip fell at the Serpent. Story Jenks and Toughkenamon retired after a fall at the Serpent.

Then came the final blow: Mike Plumb on Laurenson — the dressage leader, the favorite, and the most likely gold medal prospect — was eliminated at the Serpent.

Jack LeGoff surveyed the scene and sadly shook his head. "There was a lot of damage done out there on the battlefield," he said, while the despondent American grooms packed up their equipment slowly. No one had much to say as they made their way back to the stables.

Bruce caught up with Carol and Buck, who had been riding back and forth on the press officer's golf cart all day to keep the youngster occupied. "How's Might Tango?" was Carol's first question.

"He's going to be all right, but I'm going back to look at him."

They walked together up to the barn.

The scene there was that of a field hospital. Subdued riders and grooms worked on their horses, while the veterinarians moved from stall to stall to do what they could. Never before had so many personal disasters overtaken the team and their friends. So many good horses had come to grief, exhausted by the demands of the competition and the relentless heat.

Bruce felt everyone saying, "My God, can you *believe* that Might Tango is in first place?" He seemed to be the only one to have known that the horse had the potential. Dr. Hazzard, Mary's father-in-law, came by, remarking: "I'm not surprised that *you* got round, Bruce, but I'm goddamned surprised you got that big gray horse around! Whether you like it or not, I would never have taken that horse over a course like that — he wouldn't have gotten around if anyone else had been on him."

Might Tango was still on his feet, but his head was low and his muscles twitched from time to time. He was too exhausted to be interested in anything, spent to the last gram of strength by his supreme effort.

Bruce went into the American tack room and found LeGoff sitting with his riders, speaking to each in turn and praising them and thanking them for their endeavors. When he was through he dismissed them with orders to go to the traditional ball and to smile.

The casualty lists were long, and the form book had gone out the window. Bruce and Might Tango were in first place; Ralph Hill and Sergeant Gilbert were a no less astonishing second; Mark Ishoy of Canada on Law and Order was third; Helmut Rethemeier of Germany on Ladalco was fourth; Caroline Treviranus on Comic Relief was fifth; John Watson, Ireland's sole entry, was sixth; Richard Meade on Bleak Hills was seventh; and Carol Harrison of New Zealand, last in dressage on her Anglo-Arab, Topic, had dramatically pulled up to eighth. Lucinda Prior-Palmer and Village Gossip, in spite of the fall, had posted the fastest time of the day and were in eleventh place with 138.8 penalties. The Canadian team, to everyone's surprise, had a commanding lead. They were the only team to have gotten all four riders around.

Horses stood in bandages. A Dutch horse who had been ill before he even started was in very poor shape, and one of New Zealand's horses was going berserk in his stall from the pain of an injured hock. Many horses were flat in their stalls, oblivious to the confusion. Might Tango lay down and went fast asleep.

The riders drove back to the hotel to rest and clean up for the party, leaving the grooms and veterinarians to watch over the horses. Most of the stable workers stayed up all night. Bruce and Carol checked back into the barn when they left the party and found Might Tango still asleep and Jane sitting beside his door in a deck chair in case he needed anything. Bruce said goodnight and drove off with Carol to get some sleep himself.

At 2 A.M. Jane finished helping one of New Zealand's grooms with a horse who had got his legs stuck up against the wall and had to be rolled over. She decided to go out to the all-night snack stand just outside the door to get a cup of coffee to help her stay awake. As she waited for her coffee she heard a great clattering coming from the barn and ran back inside. Might Tango had woken up and missed her. He had stuck his head out of the door and had picked up her deck chair and was banging it against the wall in protest.

Jane laughed out loud. "That's just like you, Ducky," she scolded. "Now I know you'll be all right. You're your old self." She patted his neck and took the chair gently away from him.

What follows are drawings of every fence on the cross-country course, in sequence. Bruce's comments appear after each fence.

Entries in italic type show where and to whom the faults happened. The horse's name is followed by the name and country of its rider.

Where an option of routes was offered, alternative choices are marked on an accompanying diagram.

The Kentucky World Championships Course

1. Logs & Shrubs
Height 1.20 m. (3 ft. 11 in.)
Width 1.80 m. (5 ft. 11 in.)

No faults

A standard first fence, it helps the horse get off the ground because it slopes away from the horse. It is a proper fence with which to start a course.

2. Water Trough
Height 1.15 m. (3 ft. 9 in.)
Width 1.70 m. (5 ft. 7 in.)

One refusal: *Autumn Haze, Eddi Stibbe, Holland*
Sunrise, Liz Ashton, Canada
Arpegio, Alberto Gonzalez, Argentina

A square oxer, a very solid fence that calls for the horse to get up into the air. A square, solid wall in show jumping is inclined to get one or two stops. The horse could not see the water in the trough until he was about to take off, which must have given him a surprise. Perhaps the riders who had problems here thought, "Well, we're not really on course yet," and suddenly they arrived at a bad spot on a very square fence and the horses put on the brakes. Horses do get taken by surprise.

3. & 4. Park Pavilion
Height 1.20 m. (3 ft. 11 in.) both

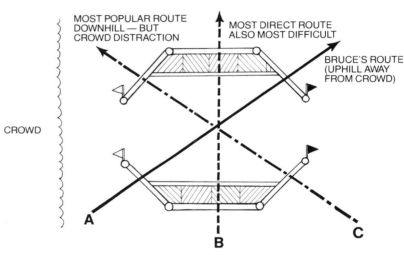

FENCE 3:
Eliminated: *Arpegio, Alberto Gonzales, Argentina*
Refused and fell: *Kielin, Carlos Rawson, Argentina*
Bandolier, Joanne Bridgman, New Zealand
One refusal: *Jacapo Red, Rudolfo Tejada, Guatemala*
FENCE 4:
No faults

These two fences gave riders the option to go down the middle, or to go slightly uphill or downhill; in the approach the riders had to evaluate the crowd location. The major problem was the adjustment necessary because the horses would be jumping from the light into the dark. The efforts required to jump straight down the middle were substantial, and the distance inside between the two elements required a very long stride. The distances on the diagonal lines from left or right were correct. I chose to jump from the left because I wanted to turn my horse away from the distraction of the crowds and make him look only at the fence.

154

5. Diamonds

Height 1.15 m. to 1.45 m. (3 ft. 9 in.
    to 4 ft. 9 in.)

*One refusal: Jacapo Red, Rudolfo Tejada, Guatemala
             Davey, Andrew Hoy, Australia*

You had to be accurate over this one because it was not a natural-looking fence. Diamonds are attractive to look at as they are architecturally fun to create, but I do not think you get a particularly good feeling when your horse jumps one. It is hard for horses to focus on such fences because there are too many bits for them to look at, so they do not really make sense in galloping country.

6. & 7. Jenny Lane Crossing

Two stone-faced banks
Height 1.15 m. (3 ft. 9 in.)
Width 1.50 m. (4 ft. 11 in.)

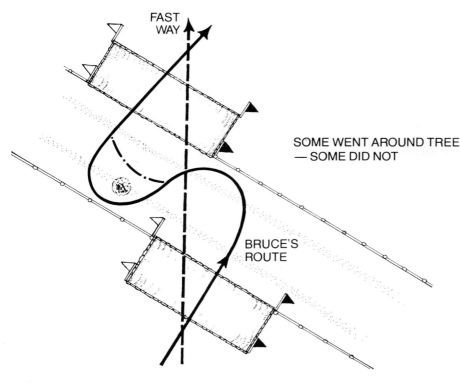

No faults

These two banks were offset on either side of the lane, posing an accuracy question for the rider and a judgment question as to whether or not you wanted to take a chance. The direct way (a) was preferred by many and rode well, but I chose *not* to take the chance of angling across the two — I jumped in straight, turned, and jumped out. I was on a very young horse, and it was easier for him this way. As it was, he banked them [jumped onto the top and off again instead of jumping clean over], so I was glad I had approached them in the way I did.

8. & 9. Sinkhole
Height 1.10 m. to 1.20 m. (3 ft. 7 in.
to 3 ft. 11 in.)

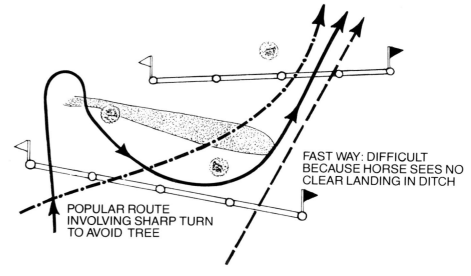

FAST WAY: DIFFICULT
BECAUSE HORSE SEES NO
CLEAR LANDING IN DITCH

POPULAR ROUTE
INVOLVING SHARP TURN
TO AVOID TREE

Eliminated: *Jacapo Red, Rudolfo Tejada, Guatemala*
One refusal: *Topic, Carol Harrison, New Zealand*
                Comic Relief, Caroline Treviranus, USA
                Cafayate, Lt. Pedro Mercado, Argentina

This was the most difficult fence on the course if taken on a straight line.
Most people ended up taking the long way through on the left. When I
first looked at it I was interested in jumping through on the right-hand
side, and had I been on Irish Cap, I would have done so. It was a hard
fence, a technical fence; you had to have your speed right, your balance
right. The horse had to be very bold and clever.

A vertical fence with a drop behind like this one and no apparent
landing is a lot for a horse to look at. It was a reasonable fence, but it
was in shadow under the trees and also it had a crowd around it. It took
some thought — Roger [Haller] likes to make riders think.

10. Giant's Table
Height 1.20 m. (3 ft. 3 in.)
Width 2.00 m. (6 ft. 7 in.)

No faults

A nicely creative form of a familiar type of fence.

11. a, b, c Kennels
Height of each element 1.15 m.
 (3 ft. 9 in.)
Height of Kennel 1.30 m. (4 ft. 3 in.)

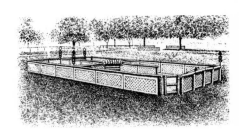

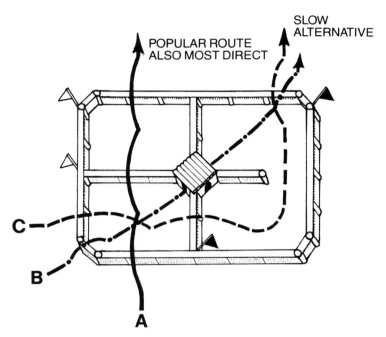

Refused and fell: *Bally Cor, Tad Coffin, USA*
One refusal: *Marcus Aurelius, Mary Anne Tauskey, USA*
                      Autumn Haze, Eddi Stibbe, Holland
                      Cafayate, Lt. Pedro Mercado, Argentina

This was a clever fence and a difficult fence. A triple bounce like this, which means that the horse must land and take off each time without the benefit of a stride in between, is a big effort. It did get the horse sharp and quick and awake before the Fort, which was also a bounce. It was an introduction. It rode just fine. I felt, however, that if you came in with a lot of horse, by the time you had jumped through the out element the horse had lost most of his momentum.

12. Stack of Logs
Height 1.20 m. (3 ft. 3 in.)
Width at top 2.00 m. (6 ft. 7 in.)
Width at base 3.00 m. (9 ft. 10 in.)

No faults

A fill-in fence that anyone could jump. It proves nothing. It's just part of the scenery.

13. Old Fort Lexington
(Cabins and Shed)
Height 1.15 m. (3 ft. 9 in.) to
   1.30 m. (4 ft. 3 in.)
Width 1.80 m. (5 ft. 11 in.) to
   2.40 m. (7 ft. 10 in.)

Fell: Kielin, Carlos Rawson, Argentina

A straightforward approach fence. I liked the choice of the cabins — it was ingenious. I certainly never expected Might Tango to bank it! Many jumped the right-hand cabin, which was in a straight line to the Fort — I liked the middle one, thinking it was easier for my particular horse.

14. a, b, c, d Old Fort Lexington
(Bank)
Height of bank 1.10 m. (3 ft. 7 in.)
Height of stockade 0.61 m. (2 ft.)
Distance between 14b and 14c 3.05 m. (10 ft.)

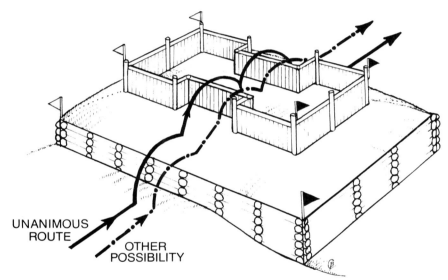

UNANIMOUS ROUTE

OTHER POSSIBILITY

Eliminated: *Kielin, Carlos Rawson, Argentina (fell for third time)*
                 Top Hunter, Mark Todd, New Zealand
Fell and refused: *Belfast Road, Martha Anne Shires, Canada (2 refusals)*
Two refusals: *Autumn Haze, Eddi Stibbe, Holland*
One refusal: *Albrant, Herbert Blocker, West Germany*
                 Abracadabra, Cathy Wedge, Canada
                 Cambridge Blue, John Watson, Ireland

A really creative fence, but I did not particularly like it. I liked the *idea* and it proved to be jumpable, but it is very hard to jump stylishly through something like this. It did not reward the horse that was a good jumper, it rewarded one that could scramble.

I felt the idea of jumping on and off was fair, but the bank itself held no purpose for appraising jumping ability — it appraised boldness and the ability of the horse to stay on its feet. Because of the effort of jumping uphill, the horses had no time to recover before they reached the stockade on top, and therefore many knocked their legs on it.

**Jane Holderness-Roddam on Warrior
at Fort Lexington.**

1. The rider is in a strong full seat, a good position in which to influence the horse and keep him going (the worst thing would be to be ahead of the horse at this point), and she is allowing the horse to use his head and neck to look at the jump he is to negotiate. She has a good secure position no matter what the horse should decide to do.

2. This really shows the incredible effort required to get up onto Fort Lexington. The horse has met a good point of take-off with tremendous impulsion. The real concern here was for the horse to get his hind legs up far enough onto the bank and not to be too close to the edge of the ditch.

3. Even with such a great effort the horse had only made it to the middle of the bank, but this places his hind feet in a safe enough position so that the rider need not be concerned with sliding off backwards.

1

2

3

Continued overleaf.

10

10. Warrior decided to put in one stride — a normal descent from the bounce on top. Most horses took one full stride from the top of the bank and then jumped off.

11. Rather than just dropping off normally, Warrior chooses to take off from the bank, and the rider has to be prepared for a sharp impact.

12. He lands well out from the base. The rider has had to sit back and support him with the reins because of the effect of the drop. This is a good example of the rider's position coming off a sharp drop fence.

4. It is still questionable here whether Warrior will take the option of putting in a short stride on the bank before taking the bounce combination on top. At this point on such an incline, all the rider can do is to stay as far forward as possible in order not to interfere with the horse's momentum and to maintain contact to assist the horse without restricting or inhibiting him.

5, 6. Having put in a short stride, the horse jumps into the bounce very comfortably. The rider is secure and helping keep him straight which is important.

7. Perhaps the rider is too far forward. Her legs have come behind the girth anticipating the take-off.

8. Warrior, like most of the horses, does not seem willing to leap off the top. Instead he jumps conservatively, not knowing what his footing will be on the other side.

9. The rider has recovered well and is secure and balanced, prepared for whatever move the horse makes on descent.

8   9

11   12

15. Old Fort Lexington

(Farmyard)
Height 1.20 m. (3 ft. 11 in.)
Width nil to 1.80 m. (5 ft. 11 in.)

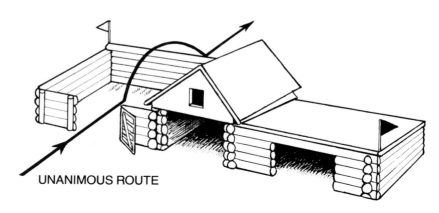

UNANIMOUS ROUTE

No faults

No problem. But after this there was an unintentional trap on the course which no one had really picked up. It was halfway round and the horses needed a breather after all that effort, and immediately following Fort Lexington there was a seductive long downhill gallop, and you wanted to let them roll. If you did, there was no place you could let them breathe again until after the Lake — and that was too late.

I remember that we talked about giving the horses a breather at the halfway point, but you really did not want to because of the terrain — you wanted to take advantage of the long downhill. This, I think, undid a lot of horses.

16. Ditch & Brush

Height of brush 1.20 m. to 1.40 m.
  (3 ft. 11 in. to 4 ft. 7 in.)
Width of left option 2.65 m. (8 ft. 8 in.)

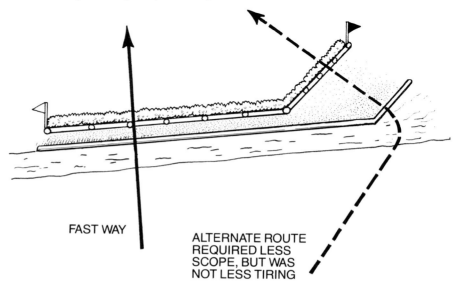

FAST WAY

ALTERNATE ROUTE
REQUIRED LESS
SCOPE, BUT WAS
NOT LESS TIRING

Fell: Abracadabra, Cathy Wedge, Canada

A nice inviting fly fence that you could bound over at a gallop. But it was extra wide and extra high, and if you felt your horse was tiring you could trot through the ditch on the right-hand side and then jump the brush separately.

17. a, b Head of the Lake
(Normandy Bank)
Width of a 1.50 m. (4 ft. 11 in.)
Height of b 0.80 m. (2 ft. 8 in.)
Drop into water 1.80 m. (5 ft. 11 in.)

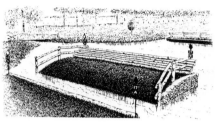

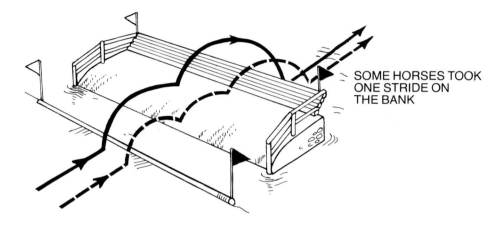

SOME HORSES TOOK ONE STRIDE ON THE BANK

Eliminated: *Autumn Haze, Eddi Stibbe, Holland*
Fell: *Warrior, Jane Holderness-Roddam, Great Britain (2 falls)*
          Belfast Road, Martha Anne Shires, Canada
          Regal Abbott, Alice Waanders, Holland
One refusal: *Albrant, Herbert Blocker, West Germany*
          Polly Ladd, Kuranojo Saito, Japan

This was a contradictory fence. The water ditch before the bank is a good idea; but a Normandy bank is designed for the rider to increase pace and jump boldly on and bounce off, and you do not want to enter water at that great a speed.

I do not think it was impossible, but it was an exhausting complex asking for very big efforts when you took into account the three big leaps that followed immediately after it.

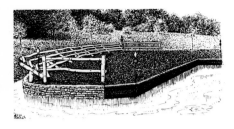

18. & 19. Head of the Lake

(Bank & Rails)
Height of 18. 1.0 m. (3 ft. 3 in.)
Height of 19. 1.15 m. (3 ft. 9 in.)

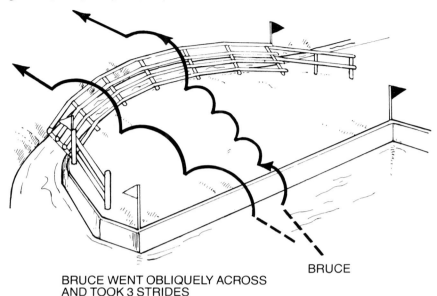

BRUCE

BRUCE WENT OBLIQUELY ACROSS
AND TOOK 3 STRIDES

FENCE 18:

Refused and fell: *Ucase, Fernando Zuviria, Argentina*
                         Davey, Andrew Hoy, Australia

Fell: *Regal Abbott, Alice Waanders, Holland*

FENCE 19:

Fell: *Bally Cor, Tad Coffin, USA*

One refusal: *Regal Abbott, Alice Waanders, Holland*
                         Abracadabra, Cathy Wedge, Canada

Not a difficult fence in itself, but it called for an enormous effort from the horses.

In my opinion too much is being made of water fences. Water in itself is a big question to jump in, or to jump out, or to jump from water to water. When all these are combined by interlocking penalty zones, I think it is pushing the horses. I do not think it is wrong to have water throughout a course, but not all the different types of water fences in one complex.

20. Head of the Lake

(Birch Rails)
Height 1.20 m. (3 ft. 11 in.)

No faults

I did not really see the point of having this fence here, only a few strides after the water. It was uphill, it was another effort, and it did not prove anything. Instead of coming on out over the triple bar as a grand finale from the splash, you had to gather the horse together again and jump up again. I felt it was unnecessary.

**Mike Plumb on Laurenson
through the Head of the Lake.**

1. At this point the horse is well onto the Normandy Bank and in a good place to make the jump into the water.

2. The horse is having a last-minute look but shows positive signs of going ahead.

3. The horse appears to be jumping to the left as if he is a little bit sceptical of what he is going to land in.

4. He has caught both hind legs and dropped very sharply into the water. Mike has done a great job of keeping as much support of the head as he has and maintaining his own balance.

Continued overleaf.

5 6

5. Mike Plumb and Laurenson have made a good recovery but need to get more organized.

6, 7. Trotting through the water, showing the depth, and the strain it exerts on the horses.

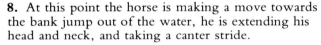

8

8. At this point the horse is making a move towards the bank jump out of the water, he is extending his head and neck, and taking a canter stride.

9. The effort of jumping out of the water is clearly shown. The horses were affected not only by the depth of the water and the resulting drag, but by the height of the bank itself. What an effort it took to get well out!

10

10, 11, 12. A good recovery and fine style over the remaining element.

7

9

11

12

21. Footbridge
Height 1.10 m. to 1.20 m. (3 ft. 7 in. to 3 ft. 11 in.)

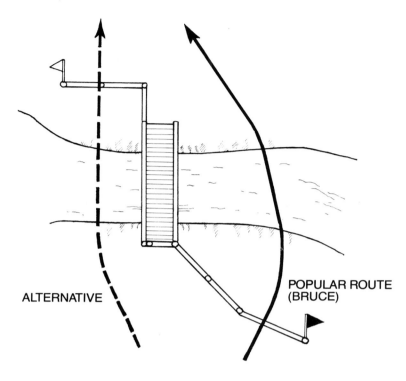

ALTERNATIVE

POPULAR ROUTE (BRUCE)

Eliminated: *Belfast Road, Martha Anne Shires, Canada*
Two refusals: *Laurenson, Mike Plumb, USA*
One refusal: *Albrant, Herbert Blocker, West Germany*
                Polly Ladd, Kuranojo Saito, Japan

After the horses have gone through all that water in the Lake, the last thing they want to see is more water. This was a hard fence and a bit of a trap. I am always wary of the small fences on courses. You *attack* the big fences and the horse generally jumps them well, but it is the little ones that catch you out.

With a ditch, the general rule is to try to jump the ditch first if possible. It is always better to go through water first and jump the rail after; but on the left-hand side of this one — the only place you could go through the water first — the fence was considerably bigger. Most of us opted to go for the right-hand side, with the hope that if our horses were going well they would continue that way.

We saw Laurenson start to give out here. Laurenson stopped twice on the right-hand side, and Mike turned him away and faced him at the left-hand side — a good example of a rider using his head to avoid a possible elimination; a good technical judgment.

22. Parallel Rails
Height 1.20 m. (3 ft. 11 in.)
Width 1.60 m. to 2 m. (5 ft. 3 in.
   to 6 ft. 7 in.)

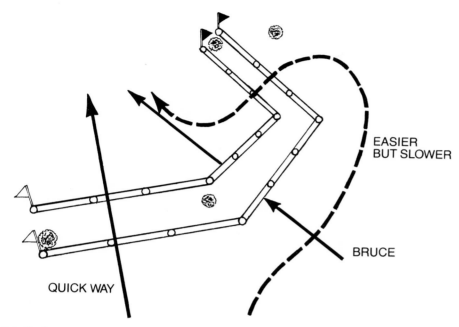

EASIER
BUT SLOWER

BRUCE

QUICK WAY

No faults

A good option because if your horse was tired you could go the longer
way around and make much less effort because the fence was narrower
at the farther end. I took the shortest route over this oxer.

23., 24., & 25. The Serpent
Height of 24. & 25. 1.15 m. (3 ft. 9 in.)
Height of 23. 1.20 m. (3 ft. 11 in.)
Width of 23. 1.80 m. (5 ft. 11 in.)

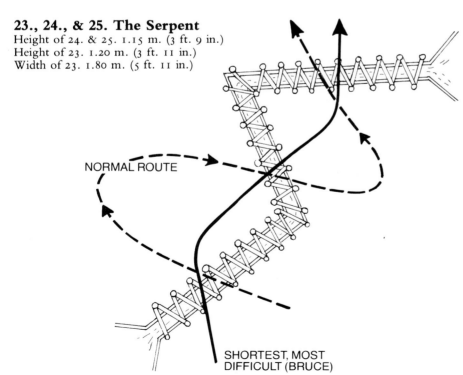

NORMAL ROUTE

SHORTEST, MOST
DIFFICULT (BRUCE)

**Carol Harrison (NZ) on Topic
over the third element of the Serpent.**

2 **1**

3

1. Carol Harrison and Topic are obviously wasting no time at the third element. The horse is clear and moving at a good rate.

2. He drops sharply into the water, hanging his hind feet on the top rail. The rider is braced on his neck so as not to hit his mouth but does not seem to be in good enough balance . . .

3. . . . to be able to assist the horse in the stride after landing.

OPPOSITE: 1. At this stage Village Gossip is jumping out of a trot and is visibly tired. He gets in too close to the take-off point and is jumping the fence at the point where there was a false ground line.

2. He has caught his right forearm, and is consequently . . .

3, 4. . . . overturned.

2 1

4 3

FENCE 23:
Eliminated: *Polly Ladd, Kuranojo Saito, Japan*
One refusal: *Albrant, Herbert Blocker, West Germany*
  Davey, Andrew Hoy, Australia
FENCE 24:
Eliminated: *Davey, Andrew Hoy, Australia*
  Smokey VI, Chris Collins, Great Britain
Retired: *Albrant, Herbert Blocker, West Germany*
  Foxie, Desiree Smith, USA
Fell: *Carawich, James Wofford, USA*
  Veberot, Harry Klugmann, West Germany

FENCE 25:
Eliminated: *Regal Abbott, Alice Waanders, Holland (third fall)*
  Warrior, Jane Holderness-Roddam, Great Britain
  Laurenson, Mike Plumb, USA
Retired: *Toughkenamon, Story Jenks, USA (fell)*
Fell: *Village Gossip, Lucinda Prior-Palmer, Great Britain*
  Gold Chip, Mike Huber, USA
  Red's Door, Torrance Watkins, USA
  Peerless Don, Peter Byrne, Australia
  Volturno, Otto Ammerman, West Germany

This was a very technical fence, demanding both riding and jumping ability. Part of the question was to pick a line and to evaluate your horse before you got there. Was it going to take more out of the horse to jump, stop, turn, jump, stop, turn; or was it better to take the most direct line possible and help the horse recover if it bobbled, which would save having to turn away and make big adjustments? In other words, how to ride as straight and fluidly as possible?

More important than all of that was the third element, which presented a false ground line if you did not turn away from the line and jump out over a front pole of the zigzag. [A false ground occurs when the horse is led to misread the take-off point because the bottom of the fence is farther away from him than the top rail, so he takes off too close and hits the top.] In that sense it was a very technical fence — perhaps more technical than anyone realized at the time it was being built.

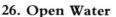

26. Open Water
Width 4 m. (13 ft. 1 in.)

Fell: *Felday Farmer, Elizabeth Boone, Great Britain*
  Bandolier, Joanne Bridgman, New Zealand

This was absolutely a gift fence. You could jump it from a halt. You just had to make sure your horse saw it. The two horses that fell over it probably did so because their riders were so elated about having gotten over the Serpent that they just galloped off the edge and never warned their horses that there was anything there.

27. Rails & Drop
Height 1.10 m. to 1.20 m. (3 ft. 7 in.
   to 3 ft. 11 in.)
Drop 1.80 m. (5 ft. 11 in.) maximum

No faults

This was a little like the Waterloo Rails at Burghley, except that at Burghley it was much more demanding on the approach. Here the approach was excellent. The strange part was the vast amount of construction that went into a fence that could basically only be jumped from one place because of the trees on the approach side.

28. Sorghum Mill
Height 1.10 m. to 1.30 m. (3 ft. 7 in.
   to 4 ft. 3 in.)

No faults

I did not particularly like the Sorghum Mill. It was very airy and did not stand up with the rest of the course; however, it was native to the area and in that sense fitted in. It's too bad it could not have been attached to a barn or something. It just stood there as if to say, "If nothing has caught you out this far — try this."

29., 30., & 31. Locust Maze
Height of brush 1.20 m. (3 ft. 11 in.)

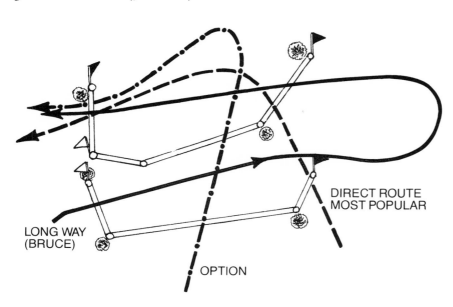

FENCE 29:
One refusal: *Volturno, Otto Ammerman, West Germany*
              Bleak Hills, Richard Meade, Great Britain
FENCE 30:
One refusal: *Veberot, Harry Klugmann, West Germany*
FENCE 31:
One refusal: *Felday Farmer, Elizabeth Boone, Great Britain*

A difficult fence since it was placed this late in the course. It would not have been a hard fence as the fourth fence, for example. It was hard because when you start throwing a lot of steering problems at a tired horse, that is when you are really taking the last out of it. To stop and turn is a very tiring factor.

The most direct route was a definite risk because the right-hand panel up at the top was very narrow, and you had to jump at an angle. The distance was good, but the angle was considerable and the face of the jump was minimal. The second option, going through the straight way, was a bit of a trap for the rider because the distance was wrong and the turn after the second fence was sharp.

I went the long way — down to the bottom, jump in, come up through the chute, turn and come down over the second and third. Jack LeGoff had gone out with me that morning to make the decision, as I could not make up my mind. I am sure it was the correct choice.

32. Hobo's Hideaway
Height 1.15 m. (3 ft. 9 in.)
Width 1.70 m. (5 ft. 7 in.)

No faults

The Hobo's Hideaway was a good fence. It had some size, and it fit into the terrain properly. It took the trouble out of galloping over the little natural ledge that was there.

33. Bank of Flowers
Height 1.15 m. (3 ft. 9 in.)
Width 2.00 m. (6 ft. 7 in.)

No faults

The last fence was like the first: super. It was there to take the horse home — not to make it fall or to pose any sort of problem.

General Comment on the Layout of the Course

The terrain was lovely, but there was no place that said you had to take it easy. It kept encouraging the riders to run on — unlike Badminton or Burghley, where you are forced to pull back because of the ground or because you are riding through the woods. Here, you had to force yourself to give your horse a breather even though everything was going smoothly. I consciously let Might Tango take a breather before the Sinkhole and before the Kennels. Later, I took a pull at him after Fort Lexington, and again before the Footbridge, and a real good breather before the Maze. I was always trying to give him a chance to take his breath.

The Final Day

On Sunday, the day of the stadium jumping, it was hotter than ever. The temperature reading was 90 degrees and there was 90 percent humidity. Walking out of the hotel was like walking into a Turkish bath. The riders, having spent the night in air-conditioned rooms and driven to the barn in air-conditioned cars, were in better shape than the horses, who had sweltered the night away in their stalls.

Bruce came to see how Might Tango had pulled through, and he laughed at Jane's account of the deck chair episode. "He's obviously feeling fine," they agreed. The gray horse looked a little tucked up through the rib cage but was bright-eyed and alert. He had come back from the brink in an amazingly short time, helped by his youth; an older horse might not have had the resiliency to bounce back.

John Meagher, the horse masseur who traveled with the American team, had been hard at work realigning tired, sore muscles, giving the older horses some much-needed relief for their stiff limbs. Mrs. Scott-Dunn, the wife of the British team's veterinarian, was doing the same for the British horses. The value of massage for competition horses had only lately been realized. It had started with Meagher, whose work on the team at the Montreal Olympics had sparked off a lot of interest among observant riders from other countries.

The horses left in the competition — only half of the original number — were led down to the track in back of the big barn for the final veterinary inspection. The strain of the previous day showed on the faces of the riders, who looked drawn and tired. One by one, they trotted their mounts out in front of the Ground Jury and were passed as fit to compete. Lucinda jogged out Village Gossip, who looked stiff after his crashing fall at the notorious Serpent. The British team were no longer in contention because two of their horses, Smokey VI and Warrior, had succumbed to the demands of the course and the heat. Only three of the American team were left after Mike Plumb's elimination. The Germans

The packed stands provide a backdrop for Bruce and Might Tango in their stadium jumping round.

still had the necessary three horses, and so had Canada. No other country had enough horses fit to continue as a team.

Might Tango did an extended trot for the crowd, back to his old show-off self; but Bruce's pride in him was tempered with sorrow for all the fine horses that were absent from the vet check.

After changing into their formal coats, the riders walked the stadium jumping course. The sun glared down on them, and several, including John Watson of Ireland, felt faint and giddy in the heat. Caroline Treviranus complained to Mary Anne that she felt terrible, and Mary Anne, who had been suffering from an intestinal virus all week, admitted that she felt equally bad.

An unprecedented crowd of over 70,000 people flocked into the stands by the stadium ring. Many could not find seats and stretched themselves out on the grass by the water jump so that they could catch the final act in the drama. The local newspapers and television had reported on every gruesome detail of the cross-country competition, and the crowd, in the fashion of crowds throughout history, came seeking new thrills.

The stadium course was long and winding and contained jumps that were surprises. A series through a large pond and a triple combination set through a deep depression in the ground, known as Pulverman's Grob after the original designer, asked for big efforts from tired horses. Bruce studied the half-mile course. "Why?" he wondered. "We jumped the cross-country *yesterday*."

The riders mounted up for the traditional parade before the jumping started, and when the decimated ranks of competitors finally filed into the ring they were met with tremendous applause from the crowd.

After riding Village Gossip in the parade, Lucinda withdrew him from the competition. "He's not in contention and he's done enough," was her humane rationale. Since the British had been eliminated as a team because they did not have the mandatory three horses fit to go on, her withdrawal did not affect the result in any way.

The first two horses had withdrawn, as had Lucinda, so Juliet Graham of Canada on Sumatra, her fourteen-year-old gray and a veteran of many international competitions, was the first to go. Sumatra had performed a dismal dressage test, finishing third from the bottom, but had been so full of running on the cross-country that it had taken four people to hold her still to get her saddled up for the start. Juliet had gone around the course and had reported back to her compatriots that it needed to be ridden conservatively — advice that had obviously been heeded, since Canada was the only country to get all four team riders around. Now, in stadium, Sumatra knocked down just one pole.

Bruce and Might Tango were the second to jump. The big gray horse was stiff, but he cantered into the ring with his ears pricked and his eyes once more on the crowds. Bruce could afford to knock down two fences and still retain the individual title, but from the team point of view he needed a clean round if America was to keep ahead of West Germany. Though Might Tango tried, he nonetheless took down two rails.

Bruce cantered out of the ring and dismounted, patting his horse.

"Do we get a blue ribbon?" asked Buck, who had been waiting for his daddy to jump.

176

"Yes, Buck," Bruce answered cheerfully. "Ducky gets a blue."

A quick check of the unofficial scoreboard showed that if Ralph Hill went clean he could tie Bruce's final score of 93.4, although he could not take the title from the champion, as a tie is broken by taking the best time on the cross-country course and Bruce had gone slightly faster. But Sergeant Gilbert was showing the effects of the previous day, and dropped from second to fourth place with three rails down.

The drama was not over. Caroline Treviranus, who was feeling worse and worse, entered the ring on Comic Relief. She seemed dazed and unsure of her way, almost taking a wrong turn; and at Jump 12 she misjudged the take-off. Comic Relief fell through the fence, throwing Caroline to the ground where she lay unconscious. Quickly the doctors summoned an army helicopter stationed nearby and airlifted the rider to hospital, where she remained in a coma for two weeks.

Jim Wofford on Carawich beat his usual jinx and pulled off a clear round, so the hopes for a team silver medal for America were still alive. But Bally Cor, feeling her age after the cross-country, pulled down one rail, and so the German team took over second place.

In the end it was the Canadians who, like their American neighbors four years before, tore up the script and threw it away. With three girls riding gray horses and one man on a bay, they cantered round the stadium while their national anthem, "O Canada," floated out over the loud-speakers and the red-and-white Canadian Maple Leaf flag rose up the

Presentation in Kentucky.

BELOW: Bruce, Buck, and the blue ribbon.

The surprising Canadians, Liz Ashton, Mark Ishoy, Buck Ishoy, the chef d'équipe, Cathy Wedge, and Michael Herbert, the coach, with Juliet Graham Bishop sitting on the ground.

flagpole to celebrate their triumph. The valiant German team rode round behind them, and, after these, the United States.

Might Tango, the new World Champion, had been wrapped in his bright red exercise bandages. He led the way into the arena for the individual presentations, thinking, rightly, that the world was there to look at *him*; a show-off who had reason for his pride. The slender blond rider in his scarlet coat on the huge gray horse with stylish scarlet legs made a splendid sight. Bruce took off his cap and bent his head, and Prince Philip, president of the International Equestrian Federation, placed the gold medal round his neck. They played "The Star-Spangled Banner" and ran up the Stars and Stripes, and Bruce remembered Burghley. He had become the only person ever to have two World Champions in his stable.

John Watson and Cambridge Blue, Ireland's sole entry, won the silver medal, and Helmut Rethemeier of West Germany, on gray Ladalco, took the bronze.

The battle of Lexington was finished, and the casualty lists were long and sad. The repercussions would be heard for years.

Bruce slipped down from his ugly duckling and took Buck in his arms. He placed the medal round the young boy's neck. He had just time to give Carol a quick kiss before he was besieged by the press.

"The facilities in Lexington were superb. The administrative aspects of the Championships ran like clockwork . . . and the courses were the most beautifully built that anybody had ever seen anywhere — and yet the event itself left most of us who are close to the sport with a sour taste in our mouths . . .

"The media is to be commended for their excellent coverage . . . They placed their cameras strategically at the most challenging obstacles and recorded both accurately and faithfully just what they saw — crashing fall after crashing fall and horses struggling to get back on their feet when oftentimes too exhausted to do so . . ."

NEIL AYER, *USCTA News* Nov/Dec 1978

". . . the excitement of seeing so many old friends reassembled, was overshadowed by a sense of the terrible error of scheduling a major three-day event in the South during the summer. The phrase that sums up these thoughts is 'the right place at the wrong time.'"

DENNY EMERSON, *Lexington 1978*

"On first inspection none of the cross-country obstacles looked unjump-able. The test proved, however, to be a Calvary for many of the horses and 22 were forced to abandon it. Nearly half the field . . ."

XAVIER LIBBRECHT, *L'Information Hippique* Oct 1978

"Whoever attacked the really not extremely difficult course at too fast a pace was punished mercilessly . . . Intelligent riding was practiced, for example, by — unfortunately I cannot think of many examples — Helmut Rethemeier on Ladalco, but also by the Irishman John Watson on Cambridge Blue, who afterwards did not require veterinary treatment approaching doping and — as might be suspected — beyond . . . The war against the horse has been rekindled in Kentucky . . . Combined training has two faces. Which one it exhibits depends on which special factors coincide at the respective events . . ."

JORG SAVELSBERG, *Crash Cross, Reiter Revue* Oct 1978

"It may be however, that there are more deeply rooted factors of more significance than the immediate cause and effect. It could be for instance, possible that riders, course builders, juries, delegates and very importantly the general public which follows the sport, have come to accept a situation in eventing in which an optimum in respect of the test set and the capability of even top class horses is in danger of being exceeded.

"Many will consider that point to have been reached when a horse that wins a world championship requires oxygen, ice-packs and much remedial medication after completing the speed and endurance phase."

Riding, Nov 1978

"The suspense lay in waiting to hear if Might Tango could pass the vet check. Alarming rumors flew around on Saturday evening about his exhausted condition after the cross-country . . . Jack LeGoff clarified the situation by drily announcing that the medications administered to the horse were strictly in accordance with the rules of the F.E.I. It must be

The controversy that surrounded the World Championships in Kentucky led to an experimental new format for the endurance trial in 1979. The competition for the Gladstone Trophy at the Intermediate level was held in the Kentucky Horse Park over a modified course. The roads and tracks phases were dropped from the endurance competition. Horses performed on the steeplechase course and then rested for a half hour before going on the cross-country course. Here Dixie Grey is checked by the veterinarians after completing the steeplechase. Tad Coffin waits to resume his ride.

noted that the American equestrian community has a great knowledge of drugs, especially in the jumping, but also in three day and dressage."

REMY RICARD, *L'Eperon* Oct-Nov 1978

"Every competition — especially a world championship or an Olympic Games — should allow people to *compete,* not just to try to get round. The spirit of the competition is *competition.*"

JACK LEGOFF, quoted in *The Sunday Times* Sept 24, 1978

"It is one thing to make excuses about why you lose, but I do not see why anyone should make excuses about why the Canadians won . . . The short answer to us 'not competing' is that 'There are more ways of competing than going fast.' If the weather and footing had been more suitable for speed, we would have planned to go faster. We rode to beat the course first, the competition second."

MICHAEL HERBERT, *The Corinthian* March 1979

"If we were surprised, it is no exaggeration to say the Americans were stunned, but that is no reflection on Bruce Davidson's remarkable effort in winning the individual title for the second time or the Canadian team's outstanding victory."

FRANK WELDON, *Horse and Hound* Sept 22, 1978

". . . here we have come full circle to the *horsemens'* real question, the question that has set in motion such acrimony and debate. 'What is an international three-day event meant to be?' If it is meant to be a survival of the fittest, mortal combat situation, Lexington certainly contained elements of such a test. If, however, that is an archaic concept, then newer concepts must be evolved to replace the old . . . that summation will be hammered out tediously and painfully over the following months as the FEI and the rest of the international eventing community weigh the lessons of Lexington and either act or fail to act on what they have learned.''

DENNY EMERSON, *Lexington 1978*

8

Afterword

Since Kentucky, the world wide eventing community has been taking a long hard look at the direction in which the sport is headed. Several dramatic changes have been suggested, including removal of the two roads and tracks phases from the endurance competition. The FEI has already reduced the speeds required on the roads and tracks and is seriously considering further changes. Bruce has his own suggestions:

"I think the sport is a proper test of horse and rider, but it can be improved. I do not think that it needs a complete face-lift at present, but I would like to see some quiet adjustments. Here they are, in sequence:

"The dressage test holds its own weight, though it would be nice to have a change of test once in a while. It gets dull always riding the same old one.

"Phase A serves as a warm-up and does not need to be too long. The slower time just introduced by the FEI, of 220 mpm instead of 240 mpm, is a good one.

"The speed of the steeplechase is adequate, but I think that the distance should be kept reasonable. I would like to see a free five minutes at the end of the course so that the horses can catch their breath and not start out on Phase C puffing like crazy.

"Phase C should be kept within a shorter distance and should be ridden at 220 mpm, so that a rider can just hack along without having to hustle.

"The cross-country is within the right limits because the quality of horses and riding is steadily improving. Yet the sport has gotten to the point where the fancy horses and the fancy riders become victims of the course. We more frequently knock each other off our feet.

"I think we have to be very careful about the number of jumping efforts asked. It is easy to number obstacles cleverly, not flagging portions of a complex that have to be jumped anyway to take the shortest way through, but one must consider how many times the horse's feet actually come off the ground. For instance, at the European Championships in Luhmühlen in 1979 there were thirty-some fences but fifty actual jumping efforts. The combination fences are obviously rider questions, but we must consider the horse's actual efforts. We have to be very careful about the number of interlocking penalty zones.

"I also do not think we should keep asking horses to jump the same type of technical problems once they have already jumped them on a

OPPOSITE: A family portrait at Chesterland Horse Trials 1979.

course. Once they jump a corner, once they jump a bounce, when they have jumped a couple of drop fences, once they jump water, I do not think these fences should be repeated.

"As for stadium, the horse should not have to face a mini-cross-country on the final day.

"Human error plays all too great a role in eventing. When a championship course is designed, whether it be at Badminton, Luhmühlen, Moscow, or Kentucky, and for some reason the caliber of the horses or of the riding is not up to expectations, or the weather takes a freakish turn, the competition often appears to be a battle using the horse.

"A tighter control of more conscientious power over major competitions as regards location and time of year would obviate many disasters."

Chesterland Farm, Pennsylvania
November 1979

Irish Cap walks quietly with the double burden of father and son after his performance at Chesterland in 1978.

Irish Cap enjoys the attention he attracts at his retirement, Chesterland Horse Trials 1979. Paying homage are Jack LeGoff, Bruce, and the three grooms that cared for the horse during his spectacular career, Jane Cobb, Ann Geoghegan, and Audrey Blood.

LEFT: Irish Cap looks every inch a champion at his retirement ceremony.

Bruce and Mr. Tindle discuss a young horse as a future three-day event prospect.